"Movies have that magical ability to transport us to a different place and see things in new ways. They can be a useful, and sometimes less painful, vehicle for gaining insight into important life issues. With Addison Cooper's guidance, adoptive families can easily choose films to help them initiate important conversations in a non-threatening manner. Building on his popular *Adoption at the Movies* blog, Cooper's new book (of the same name) organizes 63 movies into four main categories. Alphabetical, age, and topic indexes add to the book's usability. Adoptive families and professionals who work with them will find this to be a welcome resource."

—*Linda May Grobman, MSW, LSW, ACSW,*
Publisher/Editor of The New Social Worker *Magazine*

"*Adoption at the Movies* does two huge favors for adoptive parents. First, it reveals the whys and hows of having tough conversations with our kids. Second, through previews it guides us through how to best use films as conversation starters that can foster intimacy and trust, while alerting us to potential hazards. This way parents can make good decisions about what to see and what to wait on. I wish I'd had this guide from Day 1 as an adoptive parent to my children."

—*Lori Holden of LavenderLuz.com,*
author of The Open-Hearted Way to Open Adoption

"Open communication is vital to the well-being of any family, but parents through adoption may struggle to introduce the subject. *Adoption at the Movies* can help parents get past this stumbling block. When you watch a film with an adoption theme, the topic is already on the table, er, screen, so the conversation can unfold naturally. Cooper's clear-eyed assessments of dozens of films, including excellent discussion questions, should lead to many enjoyable evenings—and many more hours of healthy conversation—in any family formed through adoption."

—*Eve Gilman, Editor of* Adoptive Families *magazine*

"*Adoption at the Movies* is a well-researched and accessible resource for all adoptive families who watch films together. Addison Cooper shows how many films aimed at children are essentially about absent or neglectful caregivers, loss, and the search for belonging, and why these themes may trigger difficult feelings in adopted children. His book gives parents the tools not only to make informed decisions and to prepare before watching a film but it suggests ways in which each film can be used as a starting point for a significant conversation. It is great to read something that not only forewarns but forearms too, and which encourages families to explore themes and difficulties together and to use films as a resource. The book is easy to use, packed with popular films and appropriate to a wide age range. I wish I'd read it at the start of our journey as an adoptive family but I'll certainly be using it now."

—*Sally Donovan, author of* No Matter What

ADOPTION
AT THE MOVIES

A Year of Adoption-Friendly Movie Nights
to Get Your Family Talking

Addison Cooper

Foreword by Rita L. Soronen

Jessica Kingsley *Publishers*
London and Philadelphia

First published in 2017
by Jessica Kingsley Publishers
73 Collier Street
London N1 9BE, UK
and
400 Market Street, Suite 400
Philadelphia, PA 19106, USA

www.jkp.com

Library of Congress Cataloging in Publication Data
A CIP catalog record for this book is available from the Library of Congress

British Library Cataloguing in Publication Data
A CIP catalogue record for this book is available from the British Library

ISBN 978 1 78592 709 6
eISBN 978 1 78450 275 1

Printed and bound in the United States

To your family, and to mine.

CONTENTS

FOREWORD

Art, in all of its forms, generates a rich mosaic for thought and discussion of our shared experiences, feelings and beliefs. The art of the movie is no exception. The magical blend of music, image, and dialogue in particular can surprise us by provoking some of our deepest emotions.

Similarly, adoption is a complex human experience that at various stages of a child's development can be both full of joy and deep with sadness; an experience that feels inclusive, or one that alienates; a source of secrecy and shame or an opportunity for security and celebration. Unknowingly, an image or a phrase in a movie can elicit a response from a child that, without a safe place to share his or her feelings, can linger unresolved.

For years, Addison Cooper has been a singular voice, gracefully helping parents and professionals to navigate the abundant adoption themes embedded in movies and suggesting ways to use what is viewed on the screen to encourage open family discussions. In *Adoption at the Movies*, he has deepened the conversation with an insightful look at dozens of productions, from *Angels in the Outfield* to *Up*, carving out the thematic strengths and the challenges families might face when watching together, while providing a guide through scenes that may trigger unexplored memories or emotions. Mr. Cooper encourages us to use this wonderful platform to open critical conversations about the adoption journey that so many families experience.

In *The Wizard of Oz*, when Dorothy famously clicks her ruby slippers together and whispers, "There's no place like home, there's no place like home," we all are taken back to a time when, as children, we were lost, wishing simply to be surrounded by those who would love and protect us. When she wakes in her own bed, surrounded by concerned family, we are relieved and happy for her. We also are hopeful— hopeful that every child in need can experience a journey that although most certainly will be challenged by doubt, loneliness and fear, at the end of the day, will also be embraced by family and home.

Adoption at the Movies is a unique and valuable resource for families and one that will continue to elevate our understanding of the challenges and joys of adoption.

Rita L. Soronen
President and CEO, Dave Thomas
Foundation for Adoption

DISCLAIMERS

Movies can be helpful tools for families that want to talk about adoption. In this book, you'll find 63 films that might be helpful to you, along with some recommended discussion questions and general estimates of the age ranges that might best appreciate a film. However, you know your kids better than I do, so please use your own judgment when deciding which films to watch together and which questions to include in your discussions. Also, no book can provide the individualized guidance that you can expect from a professional therapist. Sometimes, you might find an issue too complex to process without professional help. There's no shame in asking for help, and there's no shame in asking whether you should ask for help.

Lastly, let me provide a brief note about spoilers. The movie reviews and guides in this book contain spoilers. Perhaps you have seen the films already; if you haven't, reading these reviews will sometimes give away important plot points or endings. This is done so that you can make fully informed decisions about the films that you'll share with your family. I think you'll find that the films are strong enough to retain entertainment value even with spoilers. I hope that having key points highlighted adds to your enjoyment of the film!

HOW TO USE THIS BOOK

You don't have to read this book from cover to cover. You can if you like, of course, but you can also use our classification system or one of the indexes in the back of the book to go straight to the movies that might be most helpful to you. This book introduces 63 films that can work in a variety of adoption situations, for viewers in a range of ages. The following chapters are separated by the age group for which a film is best suited. There is also one chapter that focuses specifically on Disney films, since Disney films so often feature children dealing with separation from a parent.

Within each chapter are several film reviews. Each film review suggests a specific age range and specific issues for which the film may be helpful. There is a brief overview of the plot and of some of the film's potential connection points to adoption. The reviews also highlight any particularly bright points in the film as well as any potential emotional triggers. Finally, the reviews include several suggested questions that can help you use the film to jump into adoption-related conversations. You're certainly welcome to make your own questions. In fact, I would love to hear about the questions you come up with that generate great conversations. Let me know at adoptionatthemovies@gmail.com.

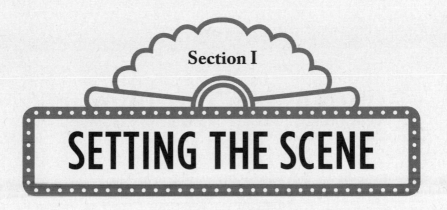

Section I

SETTING THE SCENE

Have you ever wanted to talk to your kids about something really important, but didn't know how to bring it up? Parents sometimes need to initiate sensitive conversations with their kids. Parents in adoptive families face the same task, but conversations that revolve around adoption-specific topics can be even more intimidating to start than other conversations. Sometimes, families end up falling into silence or secrecy rather than entering into the important talks that they know they should be having. These families are surprised when adoption suddenly takes center stage as a child asks an unexpected question or struggles with something they saw in a movie or heard from a friend. Proactive adoptive parents make space for their kids to be invited into healthy, open, and non-defensive conversations about adoption. In this section, we'll look at why those conversations are so intimidating and why they are so important.

Chapter 1

UNIQUE AND NOT UNIQUE

Adoption Isn't Simple

Adoption isn't simple. Like any family, an adoptive family wants their kids to thrive, but adoption adds some new complexities. Your child has a specific story of how they came into your family, and that story has some joyful points and some sad parts. Your child might wonder who they look like or why they needed to be adopted. If there are ongoing relationships with your child's birth family this adds a unique dynamic to family life, and if those relationships are not maintained that also raises a set of questions that is relatively foreign to families not touched by adoption.

Sometimes it's hard to address these complex and unique adoption issues, and at times families find themselves falling into silence or secrecy because of how difficult it is to do so. Then, families often find themselves surprised when those underlying adoption issues cause their children to react in unexpected ways to life experiences. Perhaps a scene in a movie revolves around an orphanage, a grade-school assignment asks children to examine their family trees for shared genetic traits, or a classmate asks an indelicate question, and in response to these, your child breaks down crying, withdraws, or gets surprisingly upset. Parents try their best to redirect the reaction or to respond in an appropriately comforting way but may be left inwardly wondering how to predict when these reactions will come up and perhaps even wondering if there's a way to move from addressing them reactively to addressing them proactively. I think there is!

Adoption themes are present in many films. Superman, Princess Leia, and *Kung Fu Panda*'s Po were all adopted. Antwone Fisher, Angela Tucker, and Tigger all took journeys in search of their birth families. Films like *Martian Child*, *The Blind Side*, and *Big Daddy* show adults figuring out what it means to be a parent to someone who spent the first years of their life somewhere else. With intentionality and guided discussions, movies like these can be more than just entertaining diversions. They can serve as easily accessed roads into previously hard-to-reach conversations.

Before we jump into movies, let me share a bit of TV with you! In a Halloween-themed episode (Jean *et al.*, 1991), Homer Simpson is standing in a mysterious market stall that sells curios, and is in the process of purchasing a magical monkey's paw. Homer has heard that the paw will grant him three wishes, and he's excited to own it and reap the benefits of ownership. He's a bit taken aback when the honest stall holder tells him that there are dangers as well as blessings. The monkey's paw, as it turns out, is cursed, and every desired thing it grants will be colored by misfortune. Instead of hearing the details, Homer just wants to take his treasured item and go.

For many, adoption may be like that magical item. People pursue adoption intending to fulfill their wishes— to become parents, to expand their family, to feel complete, to do good, and to help kids in need. As they get closer to adoption, though, they realize that adoption isn't as simple and uncomplicated as they had expected. Unforeseen challenges and complexities arise. Unexpected emotions surface with surprising force. Friends and family might not understand what they're going through. Adoptive parents might think privately, "We expected this to be easy, and we're a little embarrassed that it isn't." It can be confusing and discouraging.

You're not in the same situation as Homer. Adoption isn't cursed, and you're not helpless—but, unlike Homer, it would make sense to take some time to understand the complexities of the treasure you're hoping to add to your life!

Adoption has aspects that are familiar to most parents and aspects that are unique to adoption. In some ways, families formed through adoption are like any other family. All families have similar needs and goals. Adoptive families are different from other families because of how they were created and because of a range of parenting issues, specialized needs, and additional goals presented by adoption.

All Parents Want to Meet Their Child's Needs

Any healthy family—whether adoptive or not—strives to meet the needs of their children. The psychologist Abraham Maslow (1943) presented a helpful way of thinking about needs and development. He introduced the "Hierarchy of Needs" in 1943, and wrote that people's needs are subconsciously ordered from most to least foundational. He said that people can't achieve higher-level goals until their more foundational needs are substantially met; for instance, a person whose need for safety is unmet will not likely invest much effort in developing self-esteem. A child won't prioritize what people of think of them when they're mostly trying to make sure that they don't starve. The five levels of need that Maslow identified, from most to least foundational, are:

- physiological (survival needs)

- safety (prolonged survival)

- love and belonging

- esteem and self-esteem

- self-actualization.

Maslow theorized about people in general, but his theory is applicable to children and teens as well. Kids often don't consciously realize that their physiological needs are met— they're able to survive without experiencing a struggle. They learn that their safety needs are met when they see that they consistently have access to food, shelter, and stable parental expectations. Once that's taken care of, the foundation is set for them to view themselves as part of a family, to value themselves, to share their personality and time with others, and ultimately to become whoever it is that they want to be. Successful families enable their kids to survive, feel safe, experience love, extend love, and pursue the development of their talents. Adoptive families are no different here. Like any other parents, adoptive parents want their kids to survive, share, and thrive.

Communication as a Key to Meeting a Child's Needs, and How it Uniquely Applies to Adoption

Effective and honest communication is a key to health for any family, regardless of whether adoption played a role in forming the family. Notice how communication is important to each step of the hierarchy of needs. Children are kept safe by their parents' guidance. Parents' calming words can soothe children when they fear that they're not safe. Parents convey their love through words; children are shown and also told that they belong. Through conversations, families can help children develop self-esteem and show children how to earn the esteem of others. Parents' communication can help teenagers discern direction and find the courage to pursue their dreams. Kids watch their parents communicate with each other, which models how even difficult topics of conversation can be handled healthily, without threatening the relationship. This is as true in non-adoptive families as it is in adoptive families. Adoption is not unique here. The goal in any parenting is to meet a child's needs and to help the child thrive. All families need strong communication skills in order to accomplish this.

While all families have important topics of communication to navigate skillfully, adoptive families have some additional unique topics that they must address. Think of the uniqueness in how an adoptive family is formed. A member of one family has become a member of another family. Instead of a child being brought into this family by just two parents, children are brought into adoptive families through a process that involves birth family members, adoptive family members, former foster parents, attorneys, social workers, judges, and others. Adoption brings a very public aspect to the typically private process of growing a family.

Children adopted internationally may find it challenging to belong to a family that does not share their culture. Parents who have adopted internationally may struggle to know why or how to incorporate the birth culture of their child. Children adopted from foster care—and the parents who have adopted them—sometimes have difficult histories to explore. Some adoptees might find it difficult to process their sense of "belonging" to two families at the same time. Children adopted as infants may struggle with developing their sense of identity. Self-actualization can be hard when it's already a challenge to define "self." Meeting the need for self-actualization has the potential to be a more complex task for adoptive families than for other families.

While all families want to meet their children's needs, the process of meeting those needs might be different for an adoptive family, especially if their children have had previous experiences when their more foundational needs weren't met. Maslow's Hierarchy of Needs can outline the progression of goals for children in all families, but children who have been adopted may have different or additional tasks to accomplish in order to meet those goals. For instance, children adopted from foster care have often experienced abuse or neglect. These children spend the first few formative years of their lives learning from experience that their safety needs are not guaranteed to be met. While adoptive families are eager for the children to feel a sense of love and belonging, the children may first need their parents to address the more foundational needs of safety and survival.

Children adopted internationally, or adopted domestically as infants, might struggle in their pursuit of self-actualization goals as questions of identity and history may arise in their teenage years. Adoptive families need to be able to talk about all of these topics, but it can be intimidating. These conversations are emotionally charged, and adoptive parents often haven't had or heard similar conversations before. For adoptive families, meeting a child's needs certainly involves being able to talk openly about adoption issues. What will the conversations be about?

A Unique Task Facing Adoptive Families

These conversations aren't unmapped! Adoption experts Deborah N. Silverstein and Sharon Kaplan (no date, but drawing from work originally published in 1982) identified seven core issues that are relevant to every person touched by adoption:

- Loss

- Grief

- Rejection

- Guilt and Shame

- Identity

- Intimacy and Relationships

- Control and Mastery.

They say that adoptees, adoptive parents, and birth parents feel each of these issues profoundly. At first, some people might see the relevance of these issues to birth parents as more obvious than their relevance to adoptees and adoptive parents. Let's look at how these issues might be felt by adoptees and adoptive parents. Adoptees often lose access to elements of their history and may fear abandonment. They might grieve not "fitting in" with their adoptive family or grieve the loss of contact with their birth family. They might feel rejected by their birth family or guilty for the circumstances surrounding their adoption. They might feel ashamed of being different from some of their peers or might question their identity. These issues can impact their relationships with others and can leave them feeling as though they haven't had control over some very important aspects of their lives.

Adoptive parents may feel a sense of loss or grief connected to infertility or because they had a "dream situation" that didn't come to pass. Adoptive parents may fear rejection by their adopted child or by society. Their relationships with friends, family, and each other can be affected by their feelings regarding adoption. Some feel guilty for the circumstances that led them to adoption. Adoptive parents may struggle to answer the question, "Are we really parents?" The process of pursuing adoption can be stressful. Adoptive parents often feel powerless in the pursuit of adoption.

All of these challenges are unique to adoption. They're made even more challenging because they're hard to talk about. They might even feel unmentionable—after all, aren't adoptive parents supposed to be overjoyed? Aren't adopted kids supposed to feel grateful? Do adoptive parents have permission to have some anxiety? Is it safe for kids to bring up their unsettled feelings about adoption? It's no wonder that it is sometimes tempting for families to keep silent about these fears and to hope that no one will notice that there is a real struggle going on.

Because these uncomfortable issues are unique to adoption, adoptive parents are often uncertain of how to respond to them. Even after an adoption is completed, the particular challenges of adoption are still present for adoptive parents and for their children, and once the adoption is completed, therapists and social workers often go away leaving adoptive parents to their own skills and knowledge to discuss the topics that come up. In any family, effective and open communication is key to the healthy relationships that can successfully navigate complex and emotionally loaded situations. That's true for adoptive families as well, but because some issues don't show up outside of adoption, adoptive parents are facing them for the first time when they surface in their homes. Because the issues are unique in their life experiences, adoptive parents and their children might not have models of how to talk about them. This can leave them unsure of how to start healthy, open conversations about these issues.

Sometimes parents respond with defensive claims that the issues aren't present. Sometimes their response never comes because the issues go unidentified and are only felt as vague anxiety and worry. And sometimes adoptive parents really wish they could talk about these issues with their partners and their children but they're unsure of how to broach such powerful but potentially volatile topics tactfully and effectively. Many times, even though a parent doesn't bring up the conversation, issues "bubble up" when a child sees, hears, or remembers something that triggers an unexpected, powerful, or painful emotional response, forcing families to react as best they can.

Which response is yours? Have you felt some anxiety in regard to adoption? Have you observed it in your children? Do you want to talk about it?

Movies can be a fun and easy way into those conversations. In Section II of this book, we'll look at 63 films that can provide good starting points for family discussions about adoption issues, but first let's take a look at times when adoption is surprising.

Chapter 2

WHEN ADOPTION SURPRISES YOU

It can happen when you're not expecting it. A scene in a movie, a conversation at the store, or a classroom project about heredity can bring adoption to the forefront of your child's mind. Your child might ask you the question that they're pondering, or they might keep it quietly inside, trying to work out their feelings on their own. It is quite likely that your child is—or will soon be—processing adoption issues.

Adoption issues can be difficult for parents to process with their children because they're emotionally laden, powerfully important, and often unique to adoption. They don't have to be frightening, though. Sometimes, the conversations are dreaded because of adoption-related issues that the adoptive parent has not yet processed; other times, the parent sees the value of talking about the adoption issue, but still fears the conversation because it leads into unfamiliar territory. They grasp the weight and importance of the conversation, and because of that, they may be very hesitant to make a misstep. Adoptive parents may find themselves avoiding conversations of which they acknowledge the importance because of just how important those conversations are.

Adoption will surprise you, and the conversations and issues will come up. Let's figure out the most beneficial scenarios for those conversations and then find ways to lay the foundations to make those scenarios most likely.

Talking to Your Kids

There are two possibilities with regard to how your child will process the adoption issues that come to them. They'll either talk about them with you or they won't. While some parents may secretly partially hope that the conversations won't happen, that's not actually the best-case scenario. It would be better for your children to talk to you about their adoption issues than for them to keep their feelings hidden inside. Mister Rogers famously said that anything mentionable is manageable (Madigan, 2012), and that's very true here.

Part of the privilege of parenting is being able to help your children figure out life—homework assignments, fights with friends, dating, and also adoption issues. These are all within your purview. If your child talks to you about their homework, you can help them understand it. If your child talks to you about their bullying friend, you can help them make a wise decision about that relationship. If your teen has a broken heart after a break-up, you can help them grieve. If your child talks to you about adoption issues, you can help them develop a healthy understanding of adoption and a healthy integration of adoption truths into their own self-concept.

Kids are most likely to talk to you about an issue when they feel that it is safe to do so. They've learned that it is safe to ask you for a bedtime snack, and so they're able to do that without fear. They're probably comfortable talking to you about homework and friends. You've built up a track record of responding to requests for an ice-cream sandwich, help with math, or friendship advice in a helpful, non-reactive, non-defensive, supportive way. If you can make it clear to your child that adoption issues fit into this category—things that you'll be able to talk about helpfully, non-reactively, non-defensively, and supportively—they're more likely to be able to talk with you about them without anxiety or tentativeness.

Two Things You Can Do to Make it Easier for Your Kids to Talk to You

There are two main ways to make it most likely that this is the situation you'll face. The first step in making adoption seem like a safe topic for your children to discuss with you is to do the work within yourself that will actually make it a safe topic for your children to discuss with you.

Remember the core issues in adoption that Silverstein and Kaplan (no date, but drawing from their work originally published in 1982) identified, which we touched on in the first chapter: Loss, Grief, Rejection, Guilt and Shame, Identity, Intimacy and Relationships, and Control and Mastery. How comfortable are you with the thought of your child asking you questions that deal with those issues, and how comfortable are you with acknowledging your own feelings with regard to those issues? Do you dread the thought of your kid asking whether they are really your kid? Is it a conversation that you would avoid or deflect with a quick comment, or is it a conversation that you will navigate with grace, confidence, understanding, and insight? Do you secretly hope that your child will never think about their birth family? If so, what's behind that? Do you have any unresolved issues of grief connected to infertility or the laborious adoption process?

Your kids are insightful and have a good chance of sensing your discomfort with these topics. By honestly acknowledging and working through your own feelings, thoughts, doubts, and misgivings, you can reach a place of peace and acceptance that will welcome conversation from your kids. They'll see that you talk insightfully about adoption with other adults and that you don't cringe when others ask you hard questions or say well-intentioned but unhelpful things about adoption.

Once you've done the work within yourself to make it apparent to your kids that it's OK to talk with you about adoption, the next step might be to work to initiate those conversations proactively rather than waiting for your child to broach the topics. Even when you've processed your emotions about adoption issues, your kids might not bring up those conversations. This could be because of their own unresolved emotions, because they're not sure whether it's OK to bring a topic up, or perhaps because they haven't started thinking consciously about an adoption topic.

In any case, taking the initiative to start the conversations reinforces your comfort with adoption conversations (so long as you are actually comfortable!). It also gives your kids an overt message that it's safe to talk to you about adoption issues, which will be congruent with the unspoken message communicated by your own inner work. Introducing adoption topics and inviting conversation tells your kids that whenever they're curious, you're ready to talk.

Even if you're comfortable with the topics and desirous of taking the initiative to start talking about them, it still can be tricky. Adoption issues are challenging not just because of their emotional weight, but also because of their specific relevance to adoption. You might not have had previous models in your life for how to start these conversations. Your mom probably asked you about your day at school, so you've got that model. Your dad probably asked you about that suitor who kept coming around, so you've got that model as well. But the adoption conversations might need models that you create. Soon, we'll look at some specific movies that can help you start and guide these conversations.

Chapter 3

TWO HIDDEN ENEMIES
OF ADOPTION
SILENCE AND SECRECY

Lurking in the shadows of your happy home are two threats that endanger the health of your adoption. They are fed by fear and insecurity, and they grow strong when they are ignored. They work their way into your home by dressing up as guards; they seem as if they will protect you and your children from pain, but they're secretly working against you, slowly breaking down the foundations of trust. Your mission is to identify and expose them, and replace them with honesty and candor.

Have you ever seen a spy movie where the bad guys steal police clothes in order to obtain access to places where they really don't belong? Wearing the clothes of trusted officials, the motives of these characters go untested, and everyone assumes that they're where they are to offer protection. But really, they're working against those around them. Silence and Secrecy are similar. We stay silent and we keep secrets because we want to avoid hurting or confusing our children, or perhaps we are trying to avoid the pain we feel when we explore issues of loss or grief. But really, Silence and Secrecy create a sense of shame and they close the doors of open communication that are important to the health of any family, and perhaps especially to the health of an adoptive family.

So, how do they get in, how can we recognize them, how can we confront them, how can we defeat them, and how can we replace them?

Silence and Secrecy enter adoptive families when families have not made peace with core adoption issues. When we are not comfortable acknowledging elements of grief or loss in ourselves or in our children we become prone to Silence and Secrecy. We believe that Silence and Secrecy will help shield us or our children from uncomfortable feelings and frightening uncertainty. We believe that they will protect us.

It might surprise you to know that Silence and Secrecy are not the historical norm for adoption in America. It wasn't until 1917 that the state of Minnesota introduced the first steps towards making adoption confidential. This was done, at least in part, to protect adoptees from the prying eyes of nosy neighbors who would expect genetics to foretell a negative future for adoptees. The intent was never to have adoption be secret from the adoptees themselves, but by the end of World War II, that had happened. Confidentiality had morphed into Secrecy.

Confidentiality vs. Secrecy

It might be helpful to distinguish between the two: Confidentiality is not Secrecy. Confidentiality is a healthy boundary that an adoptive family maintains. The family knows and communicates internally about their adoption story, and they embrace the happy and sad parts of it. The adoption story is the shared story of parents and child. The choice of whether and when to share it with others is theirs. Confidentiality is a good thing. Confidentiality communicates, "This is my story, and I can choose whether to share it."

Secrecy is different; it assumes that people will misunderstand or judge you based on your story. It comes forth when we are unwilling to acknowledge difficult parts of our adoption story and unwilling to acknowledge our own insecurities. It keeps us from talking about adoption with our friends and family and sometimes even keeps the adoption hidden from the adoptee. It keeps the names of birth parents hidden away on sealed original birth certificates. While Confidentiality says this is your story to choose how to share, Secrecy says, "This is my shame, and I can't share it with anyone."

Here's a helpful way to distinguish between Confidentiality and Secrecy. If you balk at the idea of putting your child in a shirt that says "I am adopted," that might be you honoring your child's Confidentiality. If you balk at the idea of your child telling a trustworthy friend, "I am adopted," you might be dealing with Secrecy. If you balk at the idea of posting pictures of your adoption ceremony on your Facebook page without any privacy settings, you might be honoring your child's Confidentiality—you're letting them choose when to share their story and with whom. If you balk at the idea of showing pictures of your adoption ceremony to a dear friend because you are scared they might disapprove of you, you might be dealing with Secrecy. If you hesitate to complain publicly about your worries with regard to your child's desire to contact their birth family, you're probably honoring your child's Confidentiality. If you never talk about your child's birth family with your child or your co-parent, you might be facing Secrecy. Confidentiality can open conversations, while Secrecy shuns questions and curiosity.

Timing vs. Silence

Silence is quite similar to Secrecy, but it presents as friendlier and gentler. Secrecy says, "We must not talk about this." Silence says, "I'd better hold back and do nothing." Secrecy is active quelling of adoption discussions while Silence is a passive way to the same end.

Silence isn't the same thing as Timing. Timing acknowledges that there are opportune and inopportune times to discuss sensitive topics. Silence avoids the topic, perhaps hoping that someone else will bring it up. Timing would suggest that you don't interrupt a crying friend to tell her that her shirt's on inside out, but you'll tell her before she heads into work. Silence would suggest that you don't mention it at all, because you don't feel comfortable with the thought of causing her embarrassment. Timing would suggest that you wouldn't confront your friend for hurting your feelings last week while she is at the funeral of a loved one; Silence would say you should never talk about it—maybe you'll get lucky and it will go away on its own. Timing can preserve relationships, honor the other person, and make effective communication more possible. Silence slowly chokes relationships, assumes the other person isn't reasonable enough to converse with you, and prevents effective communication.

Here's a way to figure out whether you're dealing with Timing or Silence: think of an adoption issue that you haven't yet discussed with your child. If you're waiting until a specific day, time, age, or developmental milestone, you're probably dealing with Timing, and your main tasks are to make sure that the time you've picked is a reasonable one, and to prepare for that conversation. If you can't specify the point at which you plan to have the conversation, or if you're waiting for your child to bring up the topic, you might be dealing with Silence. Silence seems more polite than Secrecy—Secrecy interrupts a conversation while Silence avoids one—but both ultimately stop healthy communication from happening.

Defeating Silence and Secrecy

Now that we know what Silence and Secrecy look like and how they get into our lives, we need to confront them, defeat them, and replace them. There are two main battlefields on which you will fight them—within yourself and in your relationships.

Defeating Silence and Secrecy within Yourself

The first battles must be fought within yourself. To confront Silence and Secrecy, first honestly examine your actions, conversations, and thoughts. Are you practicing Confidentiality or Secrecy? Are you intentionally timing your conversations, or are you waiting in a fearful silence? If you discern that Silence and Secrecy are present, you must confront them. Acknowledge that they are present. Working through the issues that allow Silence and Secrecy to exist is highly skilled personal work for the benefit of your children.

This is honorable work, not shameful work. Acknowledging that Silence and Secrecy have a presence in your life requires humility and insight. Even acknowledging that they exist is a victory.

To defeat them, learn their battle plans! Look at each of the core issues in adoption we mentioned earlier, and then consider the times when you see Silence and Secrecy rearing their heads in your family. Which issues are behind these incidents? It's possible that issues of Identity drive you into Silence and Secrecy, but not issues of Grief, as would be the case for an adoptive father who loves his children but wonders inwardly whether he is "really a dad." Or maybe it's Loss and Control, but not Intimacy, like an adoptive mother who has built wonderful relationships in her home, but who still mourns her experiences of infertility and still finds it easy to worry because of the powerlessness she felt throughout the adoption process. When you see where the battles are being fought, you can do the work that will help you win.

There are more than a few things you can do to accomplish this work in yourself. Perhaps the first step should be to contact a therapist or a support group with a specialization in adoption. They can help you develop insight and understanding into your hidden thoughts and fears and can help you reach a place of victory over Silence and Secrecy. Talking to sympathetic friends who will listen and support your goal can also be helpful. Journaling is also a good practice, as is reading books about adoption. Also, this book contains a chapter on movies that are particularly good for adults; find the films in that section that connect to the adoption issues that are most relevant to your battle and use them as fuel for reflection and conversation.

Acknowledging, finding, and addressing the issues that lead to Silence and Secrecy puts you in a spot where you can begin replacing Silence and Secrecy with open and honest communication, even as you continually work on those issues. You can intentionally choose to talk to your child, family, or co-parent about adoption issues. You can embrace your unique identity as an adoptive parent.

Defeating Silence and Secrecy in Your Relationships

The second battlefield where Silence and Secrecy must be defeated is in relationships—with your co-parent, your extended family, and, perhaps most importantly, with your child.

Do you see the people closest to you shying away from adoption conversations? Is it possible that they are honoring your confidentiality, or are they scared to bring up the conversation for fear that it would be embarrassing or shameful? Is your child waiting until their 13th birthday to ask you about their birth parents, or are they remaining silent, unsure whether they're allowed to bring up the topic?

The most direct way to know what's going on in someone else's mind is to ask them skillfully and directly. Once you've reached a spot of comfort with adoption issues yourself, you will more likely be able to broach the topic sensitively with your loved ones. Asking them about their level of comfort discussing specific adoption issues rather than asking them about the adoption issues themselves is a skill called meta-communication. It's like a couple talking about how they talk over important issues, rather than just diving into the conversation.

This might sound like you asking your child, "How do you feel about the thought of talking about your birth parents?" Or asking your spouse or extended family, "How comfortable are you with how our adoption process has gone so far, and with how we've communicated about it?" Let their responses indicate their level of comfort. If they've been practicing Confidentiality and Timing, you're free to have important adoption conversations whenever you want, and the movies in this book can be helpful tools to begin them. If they've been practicing Silence and Secrecy, you face the same tasks that you managed within yourself earlier: to confront and defeat Silence and Secrecy and then to replace them with openness and honesty.

Confronting Silence and Secrecy in others is a delicate operation. The reasons why Silence and Secrecy exist suggest the delicacy of the task—people have remained silent and kept secrets because of a desire to protect their or your emotions. It's better to offer invitations rather than issue orders. If they are uncomfortable talking about adoption issues, you can simply say, "I've been uncomfortable talking about them, too, but I've done a lot of thinking and I am ready to talk about them whenever you'd like."

You can use the movies in this book to invite your family into conversation about their own stories or about topics in relevant fictional stories. You can't force others to be open, but you can acknowledge that it seems to be a difficult topic of conversation, offer a standing invitation to conversation, and present ways for the conversation to grow organically.

Once your child or loved one is comfortable talking about adoption, it's important to make sure that the environment is well-suited to sustain the change. You can accomplish this with honesty, openness, and non-defensiveness. Don't take people's doubts and questions as personal offenses, but instead be accepting, empathetic, and nurturing. If insecure feelings or defensiveness start to well up within you, instead of venting them and shutting down the present conversation, you can address them with the tactics you've been using on the first battlefield—examine your thoughts, talk with trusted friends, and possibly consult an adoption-specialized therapist.

These are battles that you can win! To defeat Silence and Secrecy, you will want to make sure that the battlefield is slanted to your advantage. In the next chapter, we'll look at ways to make the environment in your family conducive to healthy conversations about adoption.

Chapter 4

HOW MOVIES CAN HELP

Suppose you've done the work to identify and confront Silence and Secrecy. You've examined and honed your own level of comfort with adoption issues that have been challenges to you in the past. You've discerned the difference between Confidentiality and Secrecy, and have made the shift in thought that allows adoption to be something that you can choose to talk about, rather than something that you have to avoid. You've also come to see the difference between waiting on good timing to bring up a topic and waiting indefinitely to avoid a topic.

You're inwardly ready to discuss adoption issues with your children and your family in an open, honest, non-defensive way—yet you're not sure how to start the conversations. You want to get into those conversations, but they're hard to access. You're not alone. This book is for you.

Suppose you haven't confronted Silence and Secrecy in your own life. You want to do it, but you don't know where or how to start. This book is for you, too. Movies can help you guide yourself and your co-parent into discussion and deep thought about adoption. Some movies are particularly great viewing for people who haven't adopted yet, but who are considering it.

Adoption at the Movies is for adoptive parents who want to talk openly and honestly about adoption issues with their children and their families, but who need some help figuring out how to access those conversations. Remember, part of successful parenting is navigating emotionally laden topics with your kids.

For most topics, parents are able to rely on the models that they had growing up—your mom talking to you about dating morals, your dad talking to you about financial responsibility, your parents, grandparents, or teachers talking to you about manners, filling up the car with gas, curfew, and using deodorant—and you're often able to borrow from conversations you've already been a part of.

For adoption-related topics, though, parents may not have previous conversations from which to draw and they may feel as though they're without a model for starting the adoption-related conversations. Many adoptive parents were not themselves adopted. Other adoptive parents were adopted, but were not given a steady stream of healthy conversations about adoption issues. How can adoptive parents access these important conversations?

We learn many of our lessons from stories, and films are some of the most accessible, entertaining, and sharable stories in our culture. *Adoption at the Movies* was created to help families use films as easily accessible bridges into previously hard-to-reach, important adoption conversations.

Movies can help in several ways. Some films, like *Kung Fu Panda 2,* are directly about adoption. When a film is about adoption, it can be easy for families to draw parallels between their own experiences and those of the characters on screen. Intentionally choosing films that portray characters going through similar situations or experiencing similar feelings to what your children are experiencing can open the door to conversations about those experiences and emotions.

Both direct and indirect questions can be helpful. The conversations can be accessed directly by asking questions like, "How would you have felt in that situation?" or, "Have you ever experienced what that character experienced or felt like that character felt?" But the conversations can also be accessed indirectly by asking, "How do you think that character felt?" or, "What do you think was right or unfair about the situation that these characters were in?" These conversations can feel natural, since they're just part of talking about a film that you just shared and enjoyed with your child. They can make the emotionally laden adoption topics seem less threatening by presenting them in the context of a normal, relaxed conversation about a shared pleasant experience.

Some movies, like *Despicable Me 2*, are not directly about adoption, but feature adopted characters or adoptive families. Many more movies feature children who have been separated from their first parents or from siblings. These can help to normalize adoption and other aspects of the adoption experience by subtly reinforcing for a child the fact that they are not alone in their experience.

Many of these films show the characters experiencing and expressing their grief and working towards some form of resolution. These films can be very helpful for parents who want to help their children talk freely about their feelings. Asking how a certain character felt at different points in the film and then validating your child's responses can be a very positive way to invite them to talk openly about some of their feelings. Sometimes kids aren't sure if they're allowed to express unhappy feelings about anything connected to their adoption, and movies like these are a way for you to say, "You're not the only one with those feelings; it's OK to talk about them, and in talking about them you will probably eventually find ways to feel better."

Other movies that do not specifically mention adoption still contain themes that are relevant to adoptive families and children who have been adopted, like *Finding Dory*'s title character trying to remember the parents that she has not seen for a long time. Some films, like *Earth to Echo*, feature foster kids, and children who have been through foster care might find those characters easy to relate to and easy to use as touch points for conversations about their own experiences.

Other films, like *Inside Out*, feature families moving, and while moving is a familiar experience to many children, it might be particularly powerful for kids who remember their moves that occurred in the context of foster care or adoptive placement. Because the characters in these films often express their ambivalent and painful feelings, the films can provide a way for kids to identify and share how they've felt.

Movies aren't only helpful for younger viewers. Adoptive parents and prospective adoptive parents can use films as a course of study that can be either self-directed or guided by therapists or social workers. Many films and documentaries exist that explore adoption, reunion, identity, and loss. An intentionally chosen film, paired with time for open conversation and genuine reflection, can be an effective way to invite personal growth regarding adoption issues.

It is important to choose films carefully. Sometimes movies that are directly about adoption portray adoption, or some parts of the process, in frightening or misleading ways. These can introduce false ideas about adoption and they can sometimes function as emotional triggers, causing kids to experience unpleasant, unexpected emotional reactions to the films. Many adoptive parents have been surprised by their kids' reactions to certain films. Perhaps just as often, parents are surprised by the contents of films that they had expected to be harmless; their kids' reactions aren't surprising in light of what the movie portrayed, it's just that the movie caught the family off-guard.

Using the *Adoption at the Movies* website (www.adoptionatthemovies.com) as a resource before watching a film can help you determine whether it's likely to include emotional triggers that could negatively affect your children. Parents can also choose to watch a film on their own before sharing it with their children; in doing that, you can both avoid triggers and develop a plan of how to use the film to open conversations.

You've done the hard work of thinking through adoption issues and you're ready to have conversations. Now comes an easier part: time to heat up some popcorn and pick out a movie!

Section II

THE MOVIES

Now let's put it all into practice. Here is a selection of movies that lend themselves to conversations about adoption, while also being enjoyable to watch. For each movie, you'll find a plot summary, a discussion of how the film is relevant to adoption, a description of the film's strongest points, and a mention of any parts of the film that might be challenging for some viewers to help parents decide whether a film is a good fit. Each movie review includes my estimate of what age ranges might best enjoy the film, but these recommendations aren't set in stone; you know your kids and your tastes better than I do! The reviews also suggest conversations to have after the film; each movie's section ends with a few questions to help prompt the post-film discussion.

When you talk with your kids after the movies, try to convey an atmosphere in which it is safe for them to think and say anything. By being non-defensive and open to their words, you'll help them express their feelings and process their thoughts; you'll also have a good chance of having them share their thoughts and thought processes with you as you listen. Remember that Mister Rogers famously said that anything that can be mentioned can be managed (Madigan, 2012); by giving your children (and your co-parent or yourself) the gift of an open ear, you are helping even their uncomfortable thoughts and feelings to be mentionable and therefore manageable.

As one final comment, some of these movies do contain adopted characters or adoption-driven storylines, but many of them are relevant to adoption although they are without an overt adoption connection. The "Adoption Connection" paragraph of each movie review can help you distinguish between movies "about adoption" and movies that aren't about adoption but that are still relevant.

Where to Find the Movies

Nearly all of the movies in this book can easily be streamed on either Netflix or Amazon. For the films that you can't access in that way, most can be purchased through Amazon, or (in the US) Redbox, or borrowed from your local library. Two of the short films we featured are also viewable for free online, with a link provided by the filmmakers included in this book.

Enjoy!

Chapter 5

DISNEY FILMS

Disney produces films that are loved by people of all ages, and their films tend to be watched and re-watched over the years. Disney films often involve stories that are driven by parental loss or family formation. We start our journey into the movies with a selection of enjoyable Disney films that can help your family start some meaningful conversations.

Some of the films in this section are geared towards kids while others seem most likely to appeal to adults. The discussion questions in this section explore becoming a family, themes of belonging, dealing with loss and sadness, differentiating between Secrecy and Confidentiality, feelings of missing or longing for birth family members, and identity development. Let's get the movies rolling!

Angels in the Outfield

(1994, PG, 102 minutes. Live Action. Starring Danny Glover, Tony Danza, and Christopher Lloyd)

The Plot

Roger and JP are two young foster children in the short-term foster home of Maggie. They live near the home of the last-place Major League Baseball team, the Angels, and they are devout fans. Roger, the older of the two boys, has recently been visited by his father, who is about to relinquish his rights to Roger. Roger asks when they can be a family again, and his father, using gallows humor, says, "When the Angels win the pennant."

Roger takes him literally, and begins praying for the Angels to do well. His prayers are answered when angels from Heaven start helping out the Angels from California, and along the way he and JP develop a relationship with George, the manager of the Angels. Roger is surprised and distressed when he learns that his father has relinquished him anyway—but his disappointment quickly turns to joy when he learns that he and JP will be adopted by George.

The Adoption Connection

Roger is in foster care because his mother has died and his father, for whatever reason, cannot care for him. We do not know where JP's family is, but we do know that he used to live in a car with his mother. Maggie is a caring foster parent, but is adamant that her role in the kids' life is for only a short season. The kids become special to George, who ultimately decides to take them into his home. The boys are elated and express their joy at becoming a family and having a dad. George's adoption of the boys fits into a specific category of adoption that is recognized in California as a "Non-Related Extended Family Member" adoption, which is any adoption of a child by an adult who has a pre-existing, nurturing relationship with the child but is not a relative of the child.

Strong Points

So many adults in this film come to love and care about the kids.

Roger and JP start as foster siblings, but will become actual siblings through adoption. They are able to trust each other, and they share their questions and hopes with each other, including their wishes to be reunified with their families. They are overjoyed when they realize that they will become family to each other.

Maggie appears to be a competent, caring, and comfortable foster parent. She understands her role as a foster parent, and also believes that kids in foster care generally have a good grasp on reality. She believes that every kid in care is "looking for someone to love."

George acknowledges Roger's pain, but tells him that he can't go through life expecting everyone to let him down.

Roger and JP remain optimistic in the face of painful life experiences.

Challenges

An older foster child in Maggie's home says some mean and scary things to Roger and JP, but he is ultimately placed somewhere else. Interestingly, JP breaks down in tears when he learns that that child has been moved; permanency is so important and instability can be very devastating for kids who have been in foster care.

George is initially temperamental and violent. The kids appear to have a good influence on him, but children should know that adults are responsible for their own behaviors. Kids need to feel safe around the adults who care for them.

George's initial interest in Roger is because he thinks Roger might help his team win baseball games.

Maggie has the kids sleep in sleeping bags on top of their mattresses rather than under sheets, and we're not told why.

One adult says something insensitive about parents to Roger.

Roger does have to keep secrets about the heavenly angels.

Roger has deep confidence that he will reunify with his father; he gets something else instead and is happy with it, but some viewers might be heartbroken that he doesn't get what he initially wanted. Other viewers will see a parallel to their own story here. Maggie tries to console Roger, saying that his father relinquished him because he wants what's best for Roger. Those words are not likely to soothe Roger's pain, and he admirably voices his feelings.

George tells Roger that although he is not Roger's real father, he can love and care for Roger and JP. By saying this, he honors the loss that Roger is feeling with regard to his dad, but his choice of terms and the way he phrases it might be painful to some young viewers.

Recommendations

Angels in the Outfield seems best geared towards kids of ages 7–12 who have been in foster care and have moved into, or are moving towards, adoption. Its portrayal of a loving but temporary foster home and the creation of a new family could mirror the story of kids who have journeyed through foster care en route to placement with a family friend, teacher, or other caring adult. Roger and JP have real and powerful emotions but also help each other process their situation and remain generally optimistic and hopeful.

Parents would want to be careful that the themes of abandonment (via Roger's father) or angry adults (early scenes of George) are not too emotionally difficult for their young viewers, and should also be careful that their kids do catch on that, by the end of the film, George cares about the boys for their own sake, not for what they might be able to do for his baseball team.

Questions for Discussion

- At what point did George start seeming likely to be a good dad?

- Would it be OK for Roger to miss his dad at the same time that he is happy to have George as his dad?

- How does Maggie compare to other foster parents that you know?

- What do you think it's like to become brothers with your best friend?

Annie

(1999, Not rated, 90 minutes. Live Action. Starring Victor Garber and Alicia Morton)

The Plot

In Disney's 1999 rendition of *Annie*, the famous red-headed optimist lives in a New York City orphanage. As an infant, she was left with a note that promised her parents would come back for her. Now, 11 years later, Annie still waits for her parents. Other girls in the orphanage mock her, and one tells her that Annie is an orphan because she doesn't have parents and never will. Annie remains optimistic, but also wants to escape from Miss Hannigan, the cruel orphanage director.

Annie's desire to escape is granted, at least temporarily, when billionaire Mr. Warbucks invites her to spend Christmas with him. Warbucks is surprised to find himself caring for Annie and expresses a desire to adopt her. Annie declines, wanting instead to wait for her parents' return. Warbucks agrees to offer a reward for anyone who can prove they are her parents.

Drawn by the reward, Miss Hannigan and her criminal brother attempt to pose as Annie's parents to collect the reward money. They plan to take the money and kill Annie, however, their plans are thwarted. At the same time, Annie learns that her parents died shortly after leaving her at the orphanage. Although she is saddened to learn of their deaths, she quickly cheers up because she is now free to be adopted by Warbucks.

The Adoption Connection

Annie has spent nearly all of her life in institutionalized care and continues to long for her parents. Only when she learns that they are dead does she allow herself to consider being adopted.

Strong Points

Annie's optimism gets her through difficult times. She perpetually looks forward to brighter days, and eventually her hopes are realized. Annie's perseverance and resilience mirror the perseverance and resilience of many real-life foster kids.

When Annie first comes to Warbucks' home, she is asked what she wants to do—she initially mistakes this as a request for her to start doing chores, but she is redirected. Many kids come into foster care from situations that required them to be overly responsible, and it can take time for them to learn that it is OK to just be a kid.

Even though Warbucks wants to adopt Annie, he puts her desire to find her parents ahead of his desire to adopt her.

Challenges

Miss Hannigan is an unkind, threatening, and abusive orphanage director, and she is even willing to carry out criminal acts against Annie for money.

Some characters tell Annie harsh things about her status as an orphan, which might be painful to kids who have lost parents or who have felt parentless.

Although Warbucks might have a soft spot for orphans since he lost his parents when he was young, his initial motivation for inviting Annie to his home is more a public relations reason than actual care for Annie.

When considering adoption, Annie refers to her "real parents," and expresses doubt that she'd be able to love anyone else, since she loves them so much. This does not deter Warbucks, though, who continues to be committed to her. When Annie learns that her parents have died, she quickly embraces Warbucks as her father.

Recommendations

This retelling of *Annie* seems best suited to kids of ages 8–12. Younger kids might be too scared by Miss Hannigan's cruelty and her plot to harm Annie, and older kids might not be completely captured by a kid-centered musical.

Annie could be particularly helpful for kids who had been in foster care for a long time prior to being adopted, or for kids who initially had mixed feelings about being adopted. Many foster kids will resonate with Annie's conflicting desires to be adopted and to be loyal to her parents.

Although Annie waited to be adopted until she knew that her parents were dead, adoptive parents could skillfully explore what other issues might make it hard for a kid to allow themselves to be OK with being adopted.

Because of Miss Hannigan's cruelty, the rapidity of the adoption, Warbucks' initial mixed motivations for taking in Annie, and Annie's steadfast refusal to be adopted unless her parents are actually dead, this might not be a good choice for kids who are still somewhat uncomfortable with being adopted; it seems better as a tool for reflective discussion after a child has reached a sense of peace about their adoption.

Questions for Discussion

- Why didn't Annie want to be adopted at first? What are some other reasons that might make kids hesitant to be adopted?

- What made Miss Hannigan such a bad caregiver? Have you ever had any caregivers who were almost as bad as her?

- How happy do you think Annie will be now that she's been adopted by Mr. Warbucks? What will be the best thing about that for her?

- How did Annie keep her hope during her hardest times?

- If you wrote a song about your life, what would it be called? How would it go?

Big Hero 6

(2014, PG, 102 minutes. Animated. Starring
Scott Adsit and Ryan Potter)
Awards: 2015 Adoption at the Movies Awards
Best Animated Movie and Best Movie

The Plot

Teenage prodigy Hiro and his older brother Tadashi have been raised by their Aunt Cass since the death of their parents. Hiro invests himself in illegal betting on robot fights, but his brother challenges him to apply to the technological institute at which Tadashi has been working.

When visiting the school, Hiro meets Baymax, an inflatable healthcare robot that Tadashi has invented. Hiro is inspired to join the school. Shortly after he is accepted, an explosion at the school kills Tadashi. Hiro is depressed and grieving, but after he accidentally activates Baymax he begins to believe that the explosion that killed Tadashi might not have been accidental. Hiro and Baymax join with four of Tadashi's friends to form a superhero squad and pursue the mysterious figure that they believe to be behind the explosion. Along the way, Hiro must decide whether to act upon the angry feelings that he has about his brother's death or to act in a way that will honor his brother's legacy.

The Adoption Connection

Hiro and Tadashi have been raised by their aunt. When Tadashi dies, Hiro must process another painful loss but is able to remember Tadashi through the kind robot that Tadashi programmed.

Strong Points

Aunt Cass communicates her love for Hiro and Tadashi, even when they get into trouble.

Baymax wisely observes that connecting with friends could help Hiro get through his sadness.

Baymax sacrifices himself for Hiro, but Hiro must first give Baymax permission of sorts; this is the third traumatic loss that Hiro has experienced, and this one he must agree to. He has grown enough in order to be able to let Baymax go. Later, he is able to rebuild Baymax and, as the film ends, he has his robotic friend back again.

Challenges

Tadashi unexpectedly dies in a violent explosion, which might be very scary or sad for some young viewers.

As a parallel to Hiro's loss of Tadashi, a villain is motivated to evil actions by the apparent loss of a loved one.

Recommendations

Big Hero 6 seems most likely to be good for kids of ages 7–16; the explosion that kills Tadashi could scare younger kids. The film explores how a teenager deals with loss. Depression and then anger are his first responses, but through friends he finds healing, and he is able to honor the memory of his brother while moving forward in his own life.

After watching this one, consider talking with your kids about the losses they've experienced, the feelings they've had about those losses, and how they want their lives to be informed and inspired by the positive memories connected to the people and things they've lost. Your kids might also want to mention the things that they have not lost, and that is OK too, but it can also be helpful to let them know that it is OK to acknowledge and remember things that have been lost and that doing so does not necessarily convey a lack of gratitude for what they have.

Questions for Discussion

- When you are very sad, what helps you recover?

- What is the difference between "getting over" sadness and "getting through" it?

- How did Hiro avoid going from sadness to revenge? Why was it important that he did not take out revenge on Callahan?

- Which losses in your life do you mourn? How do they affect you? How can the memories of those people, places, or things inform or inspire you? How can you carry the good with you?

Chimpanzee

(2012, G, 77 minutes. Documentary. Narrated by Tim Allen)

The Plot

In a vibrant rainforest in Côte D'Ivoire, a small and close-knit tribe of chimpanzees tries to survive. They teach their young how to use tools to catch termites and to crack nutshells. Oscar, a very young chimpanzee, is constantly with his mother, Isha, who feeds and teaches him. Oscar's tribe seems to be doing well under the leadership of an adult male named Freddy. However, because resources are limited, Freddy's tribe feuds with a larger neighboring tribe led by Scar.

One battle leaves Isha separated from her tribe, and the film suggests that she was most likely eaten by a leopard. This leaves young Oscar confused and alone. He is unable to fend for himself and rapidly loses weight. Although he approaches other females in the group, they drive him away. Finally, he finds an unlikely provider in Freddy, who takes care of Oscar, feeds him, and even lets Oscar ride on his back. This paternal relationship is very surprising and beautifully altruistic.

The Adoption Connection

After losing his mother, Oscar struggles without success to fend for himself. He is too small and too young to make it on his own. Freddy begins to nurture Oscar, and the film's narrator doesn't shy away from using the language of adoption. Freddy has adopted Oscar; by carrying Oscar on his back, he is acting in a way that typically only mothers act towards their own young.

Duties to the tribe sometimes take Freddy's attention away from Oscar, and the narrator suggests that Oscar might feel this as the loss of another parent, however, the film ends with a report that the relationship between Freddy and Oscar continues to grow.

Strong Points

Oscar finds loving, nurturing care from his mother. Later, although it seemed unlikely, he finds a nurturing parent in Freddy. This film appears to have captured a real-life, animal-kingdom adoption.

The film is beautifully shot and cleverly narrated.

It's heartwarming to see young chimpanzees learn how to hunt from their parents—although it might be disturbing to see that they hunt other monkeys.

Challenges

Isha is a loving, nurturing, and patient mother; we see her nursing a very young Oscar. Young viewers might cry when they learn that she has likely died.

The monkeys are driven from their home, which could be triggering for kids who lost a home when they were taken into foster care.

Recommendations

Although it might be hard for young viewers to realize that Isha is gone, this film could be helpful for young people who were adopted and have positive memories of their birth parents. *Chimpanzee* provides a story that mirrors their own—a parent who loved this child is lost; another adult comes to lovingly serve as this child's parent.

This film should be good for most kids of ages 7 and up; parents will want to be nearby to process any sadness that arises during scenes in which Oscar is confused, alone, and rejected.

Questions for Discussion

- What did you like best about Isha as a mother?

- How do you think Oscar feels with Freddy? How do you think Freddy feels with Oscar?

- Try to imagine these questions from Oscar's perspective: In what ways is Freddy like Isha? In what ways are they different?

- In what ways is Freddy taking care of Oscar like our adoption? In what ways is it different?

- What needs are parents supposed to meet for their kids?

Cinderella

(2015, PG, 105 minutes. Live Action. Starring Lily James, Cate Blanchett, and Helena Bonham Carter)

The Plot

Ella has been taught by her parents to be good and kind. When her mother falls ill and dies, she and her father comfort each other. Years later, while Ella is still a teenager, her father marries the widow of an acquaintance. The Lady Tremaine and her two teenage daughters come to live with Ella and her father.

Ella's father dies on a business trip, leaving Ella in the care of Lady Tremaine. Lady Tremaine and her daughters badly mistreat Ella, banish her to the attic, and require her to complete all of the family's chores. One night, she sleeps by the fire in order to keep warm, and wakes with cinders on her face; her stepmother and stepsisters mockingly dub her "Cinderella" and continue to mistreat her.

While in the woods, Ella unknowingly befriends the prince. He later creates a party to which all the maidens in the kingdom are invited; he is hoping to find and marry Ella, although he does not know her name. From here, it's the story you've known since childhood.

Ella's stepmother forbids her to go to the ball and tries to prevent her from doing so, but Ella's fairy godmother makes a way for her to go. Ella and the Prince have wonderful times together, but Ella leaves before the stroke of midnight, so the Prince goes out looking for her. Although Lady Tremaine tries to stop them from meeting, they find each other. Ella forgives Lady Tremaine, but Lady Tremaine is still sent out from the kingdom, and Ella and the Prince live happily ever after.

The Adoption Connection

Ella loses her mother, and then her father. She is taken into the care of her stepmother, but her stepmother never considers her a daughter, and near the end of the film Ella exclaims that Lady Tremaine has never been her mother and never will be.

Although there is no formal mention of adoption, the story might connect to fears that foster or adoptive children might have about not being accepted by their new families.

Ella transitions from her family of origin to her abusive stepfamily, and then to a new family that she will create with the Prince.

Strong Points

Ella is continually kind and courageous, as her mother taught her to be, even in the face of cruelty.

After being through hard times, Ella finds a home where she is loved for who she is.

Challenges

Ella's stepfamily is unnecessarily and perhaps unrealistically cruel and emotionally abusive.

Both of Ella's parents die, as does the Prince's father.

Recommendations

This retelling of *Cinderella* might be helpful for teenagers who have been in multiple home situations before arriving in a healthy adoptive home. It could provide a way for teens to talk about the emotional abuse and loss that they've experienced.

It seems like this one would best be shared by teens and parents together, rather than teens alone, and it doesn't seem like a good choice for younger kids. It's helpful for affirming that emotional abuse is a legitimate form of abuse, for acknowledging that losing a loved one is very sad even if it is followed by happier times, and for offering hope that those happier times may still come.

Questions for Discussion

- What was the worst thing that Lady Tremaine or her daughters said to Ella?

- How did Ella remain a kindhearted person in the face of the abuse she experienced?

- On her way out the door, Ella tells Lady Tremaine, "I forgive you." Why do you think that was included in the film? How will it help Ella to have done that?

- Have you ever lived in a home that felt like Lady Tremaine's home?

- What do you wish for your future?

Finding Dory

(2016, PG, 97 minutes. Animated. Starring Ellen DeGeneres, Albert Brooks, Hayden Rolence, and Ed O'Neill)

The Plot

A year after helping the clownfish Marlin rescue his son Nemo, the forgetful blue tang fish Dory starts remembering flashes of her own childhood, and remembers that she was swept away from her parents. Although she has found a sense of family with Marlin and Nemo, she remembers that she used to live near California. Going only on that, Dory becomes determined to find her parents, but her quest will be very challenging because of her pervasive short-term memory loss, which generally keeps her from remembering anything for longer than a few seconds. Because Marlin remembers how bad he felt when Nemo was lost, he agrees that he and Nemo will accompany Dory as she tries to find her parents.

Along the trans-oceanic journey, Dory remembers more and more about her childhood. She becomes separated from Marlin and Nemo, but eventually reaches the aquarium where she was born. In the aquarium, she enlists the help of old and new friends to explore many exhibits in an attempt to find her parents. Although she reunites with Marlin and Nemo, and finds a community of blue fish like herself—even some who know her parents—her parents are not in the aquarium, and she is told that it is believed that her parents died trying to find her.

Dory becomes separated from Marlin and Nemo again and finds herself in the open ocean, where she remembers something her parents told her when she was a child about how to find them if she ever got lost. She finds her parents, who have been steadfastly working to find her ever since they were separated. Dory is happy to be with her parents, but remembers that Marlin and Nemo have been separated from her; she declares that Marlin and Nemo are also family to her, and so she leaves her parents to find Marlin and Nemo.

Eventually, Dory manages to gather Marlin, Nemo, her parents, and some other friends together, and they decide to start a new, shared life. As the film ends, Dory is surrounded by her parents and the friends who have also become family to her.

The Adoption Connection

Dory lost her family after being swept away by an undertow. She has a hard time remembering them, and feels guilty for having lost them. At one point, she acknowledges that she does not remember where she grew up. She does believe that she'll still recognize her parents since they will look like her. She expresses that she greatly misses them, and decides that she must find them. She wonders whether they will still love her, since she feels responsible for losing them, but she finds that they have been waiting and longing for her return.

Viewers who have been adopted or who have experienced foster care may resonate with many of Dory's feelings: longing for birth parents, a feeling of guilt about the circumstances that led to their separation from birth parents, a sense of a loss of control, a sense of confusion and chaos, and dreaming of a happy reunion.

When Dory does find her parents, she lets them know that Marlin and Nemo have become her family as well, and together they craft a new understanding of family that includes everyone who has come to love and care for Dory.

Strong Points

Marlin and his son Nemo remember what it was like to be separated from each other, and this empathy helps them support Dory in her quest. It's always good to see a person's quest for reunification be supported by those they love; in *Closure*, Angela is accompanied by her extended adoptive family; in *Rio 2*, Jewel is accompanied by her husband and kids. *Finding Dory* captures that support as well.

Finding Dory isn't a story about adoption but, like folks who have been adopted (perhaps especially adopted from foster care), Dory has been swept away from one family into another and she longs to reconnect with her first family. Marlin and Nemo have not replaced Dory's parents and when she finds her parents, they do not replace Marlin and Nemo. Both groups are her family.

Dory is aware of her short-term memory loss, and wonders whether her parents will ever forget her, or whether she will ever forget them; they assure her that they will always remember her and that she will never forget them.

One fish challenges Dory, asking how she can know that she has a family if she has short-term memory loss. She replies that she must have come from somewhere, so of course she has parents, and even if she forgets their names or faces, they do not stop existing. That's an important concept for adoption, too. An adopted person's birth parents don't stop existing just because they aren't mentioned in conversation, and the fact that they do exist does not make the adoptive family any less important to the child.

Even though Dory is not constantly thinking about her childhood, the memories are all in her mind, and certain events trigger her to remember them. Some adopted people don't pursue relationships with or information about their birth parents, but then later decide to do so when they're triggered by some event in their lives.

When Dory wonders whether her parents will want to see her, her friends assure her that they will be overjoyed to see her. Her friends are very supportive. When she meets her parents, they are truly ecstatic.

Challenges

Dory wanders away from Marlin and Nemo and gets separated from them when Marlin hurts Dory's feelings with some carelessly chosen words (he tells her that the thing she is best at is forgetting). Nemo continually reminds Marlin of his unkind words.

Some kids might find it very difficult to see young, helpless Dory swept away from her parents and then wandering alone asking strangers for help. They might also find it very sad when Dory becomes discouraged and starts to believe that she will not find her parents. It might be painful when, on several occasions, Dory comes close to finding her parents, but gets disappointed at the last moment. It's very sad to hear her say that she was too late and that she does not have family. She even describes herself as being completely alone and says that she has lost everyone. The film reaches a happy ending and Dory does find her parents, but the emotional rollercoaster could be hard for some viewers who have parallel experiences in their own lives.

Nemo wonders aloud whether Dory finding her parents means that he and Marlin will have to say goodbye to her. Marlin initially thinks that it will mean that, but it doesn't turn out that way.

One character unkindly suggests that Dory probably lost her family because of her poor memory. Thankfully, Dory challenges that character, saying that it is wrong to say she would lose someone she loves, but later she expresses that she feels a sense of blame over losing them.

One character suggests that Dory should just pick a couple of fish that look like her and pretend that they are her parents.

Recommendations

Finding Dory has some hard scenes involving parental loss and self-blame that could be difficult for some viewers. However, the overall theme seems likely to be helpful for kids who have been adopted: your family will never forget you, and if you have two sets of family, one does not replace the other.

Parents should make sure that their kids can handle the hard parts—Dory's disappointments and sadness will be too hard for some kids—but otherwise this one seems to have a lot of potential for kids of ages 8 and up.

Questions for Discussion

- Now that Dory has found her parents, Charlie and Jenny, are Marlin and Nemo still her family too?

- Why did Dory decide to try to find her parents?

- What do you think Marlin and Nemo felt like as they were helping Dory find her parents?

- Do you ever miss your first family? If you could choose who you saw every day, who would you see? How do you feel when your life doesn't exactly match what your dream life would look like? What parts of your life make you sad? What parts make you happy?

- Do you ever worry about forgetting people who are important to you? How can we help make sure that our family will remember everyone that we care about?

Family Activity

Collect or draw pictures of everyone your child loves, cares about, and considers family and create a display. Join in and include people you love. Include and talk about people who have been lost to you through death or distance to help show that even though adoption is unique, the experience of separation from loved ones is something that you can understand to some extent and something that you have navigated.

Frozen

(2013, PG, 102 minutes. Animated. Starring
Kristen Bell and Idina Menzel)

The Plot

The royal family of Arendelle has a secret. Princess Elsa has magical powers over wintery forces. After she accidentally hurts her sister, Princess Anna, her family decides to hide her powers; the memory is removed from Anna's mind, and Elsa is told by her parents to keep her powers—and her feelings that control her powers—under wraps.

When their parents die at sea, Elsa and Anna live out their teenage years as recluses in the castle. This suits Elsa, who is already trying to keep the truth about herself hidden, but it pains Anna, who does not understand why Elsa has become distant from her.

At Elsa's coronation, her powers are accidentally revealed. She flees into exile, leaving her country in a mid-summer snowstorm. Anna chases after her, both to renew their relationship and to bring warmth back to Arendelle. Along the way, Anna's definition of love is challenged, and she learns that sisterly love can be even more powerful than romantic love.

The Adoption Connection

Like in so many Disney movies, Elsa and Anna grow up having experienced the loss of their parents.

Elsa has been told by her family to keep an aspect of her identity a secret; they fear that her icy powers will cause her to be hated. When Elsa learns to embrace her identity and decides to let go of her secrecy, she is able to thrive. Secrecy is one of the main opponents of healthy communication in adoptive families. *Frozen* provides a wonderful picture of the pain that secrecy can cause—Anna and Elsa are initially driven apart by secrecy, not by the content of the secret, but by the simple fact of secrecy.

The film shows that relationships can be restored when built upon truth, and it also depicts a family coming together, accepting the truth about themselves and their situation, and thriving.

Strong Points

Frozen shows that the love between siblings can be one of the strongest bonds in the world. It's challenged by secrecy, but when secrecy is overcome, their relationship thrives.

The film is emotionally intelligent; one song conveys that bad choices sometimes result when people are feeling afraid, upset, or under stress.

Love is defined healthily as prioritizing the other person's needs over your own. It's good for kids to know that that's part of what their parents mean when they say, "I love you."

Challenges

Some young viewers might be saddened by the loss of Elsa's and Anna's parents and by the conflict between Elsa and Anna, which does involve Elsa's magic powers physically harming—and almost killing—Anna.

Recommendations

Frozen is the most commercially successful animated film of all time. It is an excellent, enjoyable film with gripping songs and healthy messages.

Frozen seems well-suited to kids and teens ages 5–18, and could be helpful for starting conversations about secrecy and about love. In fact, *Frozen* might be a good "first" family movie night film—the first conversation to have might be the conversation that says, "Let's decide to have conversations about adoption instead of secrets about adoption!"

Questions for Discussion

- What do you think it means when your parents tell you, "I love you"?

- Elsa's parents tried to keep her powers a secret so that Anna wouldn't be hurt, but it didn't seem to work. Anna was still hurt, but in a different way. What might have worked better?

- What's the difference between Secrecy and Confidentiality?

- If you could make a snowman, what would it be like?

- Do you feel as if your parents want you to keep any secrets? How does it feel? (This would be a good time to assure your kids that they do not have to keep secrets; this can tie in with the difference between Confidentiality and Secrecy.)

Into the Woods

(2014, PG, 124 minutes. Live Action. Starring Meryl Streep, Emily Blunt, James Corden, and Johnny Depp)

The Plot

A baker and his wife are mourning their childlessness. They are surprised when a witch visits them, taking responsibility for the curse that left the baker infertile. The witch explains that she cursed the whole household because the baker's father stole beans from her garden that had kept her young and beautiful. The witch gives the baker a series of tasks to accomplish in order to return the witch's beauty to her, and also to undo the curse of infertility. The baker must go into the woods to accomplish this task.

At the same time, Little Red Riding Hood goes into the woods to feed her grandmother, Cinderella and her evil stepmother and stepsisters go into the woods to attend a ball, the Prince goes into the woods to find Cinderella, Jack goes into the woods to sell a cow, and the baker's sister Rapunzel is kept in the woods by the witch, who kidnapped her when she cursed the baker's father. The baker's father has been in the woods since he abandoned his young son.

Many characters experience great loss while in the woods. The baker's wife dies, Cinderella learns that the

Prince is unfaithful, Jack's mother is killed, and Little Red Riding Hood cannot find her mother. Together, the baker, Cinderella, Jack, and Little Red Riding Hood form a family with the baker's new infant.

The Adoption Connection

Infertility is part of the adoption journey for many couples. In *Into the Woods*, the baker and his wife have to go through many frustrating steps in order to become parents; this might resonate with adoptive parents who previously went through infertility treatments.

Four of the main characters experience profound losses of loved ones before finding each other and forming a family.

Strong Points

By the end of the story, a family is formed in spite of—and perhaps even in response to—trauma.

Characters do encourage forgiveness to be shown.

Characters come together, promising each other that they are not alone.

Challenges

There's a lot of loss in this film that gets resolved unrealistically quickly.

The wolf sings creepily about his desire for Little Red Riding Hood. He wants to eat her, but parts of his song could be understood to be sexually violent.

Parents hit their kids fairly often.

The witch taunts the baker, saying that he has a sister who he will never be able to find. She seems to taunt the baker and his wife with their infertility.

Recommendations

Into the Woods might be helpful for parents who have been through a lot on their way to forming their family. It could be helpful to follow along with the baker and Cinderella on their journey to becoming a family and to reflect on the painful feelings that have been part of the experience.

This doesn't seem to be a good film for kids; it is scary, dark, and sad, and the Wolf is particularly disturbing. The film is recommended for adults.

Questions for Discussion

- Which of your feelings did you recognize in the baker?

- If you could go back five years and tell yourselves about your lives today, what would you say?

- What do you imagine that your future self would tell you about the future, and what perspective would they encourage you to take about the present?

The Jungle Book

(1967, G, 78 minutes. Animated. Starring Bruce
Reitherman, Phil Harris, and Sebastian Cabot)

The Plot

In this animated classic, the young human Mowgli was found alone in a basket by Bagheera the panther. Bagheera brought Mowgli to a family of wolves who loved him and raised him as their own for the first decade or so of his life. However, the jungle is now in a state of terror; the vicious tiger Shere Khan has returned and, driven by his hatred of humans, has vowed to kill Mowgli. In an effort to save Mowgli and to protect the jungle from the destruction that Shere Khan would bring, the leader of the wolf pack determines that Mowgli must leave. Mowgli finds himself journeying with Bagheera and with the carefree bear Baloo through the jungle, en route to the human village, all the while protesting that he wants to stay in the jungle.

The Adoption Connection

Mowgli has basically been adopted by the wolves; he has grown in popularity in the jungle and is well-loved. For the first years of his life (but only the first few minutes of the film), it seems that he has had a happy life with his adoptive family. However, he is sent away from the family for his own safety, and some characters suggest that he belongs in the human village because he is a human; this is where the analogy to an actual adoption breaks down. Children in adoptive families watching *The Jungle Book* might need to be reminded that they will never be sent away, and that they do belong with their present family.

The film might work excellently as an analogy for adoption from foster care, since Mowgli was cared for by a series of loving parental figures prior to finding what will likely be his permanent home.

Mowgli seems to cycle through identities: he's a human baby and then is raised as a wolf cub. When he attaches to Baloo, he refers to him as "Papa" and expresses that he intends to become a bear, too. People who have been adopted might resonate with Mowgli's efforts to establish his identity. Like many kids who have been in foster care, Mowgli fears being abandoned. He runs away in response to an anticipated transition that he views as abandonment.

Strong Points

Bagheera, Baloo, and the wolves all treat Mowgli with compassion. Bagheera saw Mowgli while Mowgli was an endangered infant and took him to safety; later, he helped him process a major life change. The wolves provided stability for the first several years of his life. Baloo provided him with fun, while also ultimately encouraging him towards safety. These characters each capture an aspect of the ways in which healthy adults nurture and love their children.

Although the film has some problems if the wolves are viewed as an adoptive family, it may work better to view the wolves as a loving, long-term foster family. Bagheera serves as a social worker. He initially brings Mowgli to a family of wolves, who love him as their own. However, Mowgli comes to a time of transition as he is brought to the edge of his new life, and again Bagheera serves to aid in the transition.

Challenges

We never learn where Mowgli's family is. There are scenes of jungle peril (Mowgli is attacked by a snake and later by a tiger). There are some scenes in which Mowgli is separated from his caregivers; he is captured by monkeys once, and Bagheera does sometimes storm off in exasperation. Although Bagheera intends to be done with Mowgli, he always returns—still, the implications of threatened abandonment or the scene of kidnapping might be hard for some young viewers.

Bagheera tells Baloo that Baloo cannot adopt Mowgli because "birds of a feather flock together." This statement might reflect thoughts prevalent in the era when the film was made, and parents—perhaps especially parents of multiracial or cross-cultural families—will want to make sure that their children don't read a negative meaning into Bagheera's words.

A snake asks Mowgli whether he has a mother and a father; Mowgli responds that he doesn't and that nobody wants him around. It will be important for young viewers to realize that this is a statement of Mowgli's feelings rather than a statement of fact.

Baloo appears to die, but doesn't.

Recommendations

The first time I watched *The Jungle Book*, I viewed it as an adoption story, and saw it as fraught with problems of abandonment. I like it better if the jungle serves as an analogy for the foster care system; Mowgli is brought in and spends many years under the care of several different caregivers who have different approaches to life and different ways of showing their care for Mowgli. They all do care for him, though, and bring him safely through dangers and his own feelings to the edge of his new life in the human village.

The Jungle Book seems as if it could be a very good choice for kids of ages 8 and up who have either been in foster care or are just about to be adopted or reunified out of foster care.

Questions for Discussion

- How did Baloo feel when he heard that Mowgli had to return to the human village?

- In what ways is Mowgli a human? In what ways is he part of a wolf family or a bear family? Can he be all three at once?

- Why was Mowgli scared to leave the jungle? What do you think his life will be like in the human village?

- If you were Mowgli, would you try to visit Baloo, Bagheera, and the wolves sometimes? How do you think it would go?

Lilo and Stitch

(2002, PG, 85 minutes. Animated. Starring Daveigh Chase, Tia Carrere, and David Ogden Stiers)

The Plot

In the Galactic Federation's headquarters, Dr. Jumba has been convicted of creating a dangerous creature, Experiment 626. Jumba is sentenced to prison while 626 is sentenced to exile on a deserted asteroid. 626 escapes his transport and instead directs his craft towards Earth, crash-landing on the Hawaiian island of Kaua'i. Jumba and Earth-specialist Agent Pleakley are sent to Earth to recover 626 discreetly, but 626 does not want to be recaptured.

At the same time, Nani is struggling as she tries to be a parent to her younger sister Lilo. Their parents died in a car accident on a wet night, and since then Nani has tried to raise Lilo while also trying to keep the family afloat financially. She has been struggling and has caught the attention of the intimidating social worker Cobra Bubbles, who tells Nani that he will remove Lilo from her care if she does not quickly make significant improvements.

In an attempt to help Lilo, Nani takes Lilo to a pet shelter where Lilo adopts 626, who has been posing as a dog. Lilo names him Stitch. He is rambunctious and destructive, but Lilo teaches him to behave and introduces to him the concept of Ohana, or family, which means that everyone will be cared for and remembered. This touches Stitch's heart, and he remembers it later when he is captured by Jumba. This leads to him working to save Lilo, who has fallen into a dangerous situation, and to him being allowed to stay with Nani and Lilo. Although he had come to remove Lilo, the social worker ultimately decides to let Lilo stay with Nani.

The Adoption Connection

After their parents died, Nani took it upon herself to raise Lilo; however, when she struggled to care for Lilo she attracted the attention of a social worker who threatened to remove Lilo from her care.

Stitch came from a dangerous, abusive situation and found a safe home with Lilo and Nani, who persevered in caring for him in spite of the destructive behaviors that he exhibited when he first came to their home. This mirrors some foster care adoption stories. Lilo is devoted to Stitch and defends him when Nani grows tired of him, saying that Stitch was an orphan before they adopted him.

Lilo struggles with the losses she has experienced and expresses a wish for someone who will not leave her. Later she says that she remembers everyone who has left.

Strong Points

Nani and Lilo are able to express their love—and frustration— to each other. They have an admirably functional relationship after having been brought into these parent–child roles by a traumatic loss.

Lilo's desire for stability and family is evident throughout the film; she needs it from Nani and tries to create it in her play with Stitch.

Although Cobra Bubbles is intimidating, and although he seems on the verge of deciding to take Lilo into foster care, he is sad about it and conveys both his empathy for Nani and his genuine concern for Lilo.

Challenges

Nani coaches Lilo on what to say to the social worker. Although she does this to keep the family together, it would certainly arouse the suspicions of a social worker—and it fails anyway.

A scene in which the social worker and Nani are arguing about Lilo's custody could be hard for some kids to see, since it does threaten Lilo's continued placement with her sister.

In one scene, Dr. Jumba tells Stitch that he is destructive and can never have a family, and that could be jarring for some kids who feel bad about some of their behaviors.

In one scene, Lilo actually is separated from Nani, but not by the social worker.

Recommendations

Lilo and Stitch captures the real emotions that would be felt by people in Nani's, Lilo's, and Stitch's situations. Nani is scared of losing Lilo. Lilo is desperate for permanency and grieved by her losses. Stitch feels lost and desires to belong. Some elements of this story will be powerfully familiar to children who remember being taken into foster care, and it could be painful for children who were not able to remain or reunify with their birth family members. With that exception, though, this film could be helpful to kids of ages 8 and up and their parents.

The film could be especially helpful for families in which a child has been adopted by someone who had a previous relationship—familial or otherwise—with the child. If you adopted your grandkids, your nephew, your sister, or your student, this might be a really good film for your family.

Questions for Discussion

- What do you think family means?

- If Lilo had been taken from Nani, how would her life have been different? Do you think they would have wanted to see each other still?

- Now that Nani is being Lilo's mom, is she still her sister? What parts of that dual relationship are hard? Which parts are helpful?

- Before you were adopted into our family, I knew you, but I had a different relationship to you. What is that like for you?

- Where do you belong?

Meet the Robinsons

(2007, G, 94 minutes. Animated. Starring Jordan Fry, Wesley Singerman, and Tom Selleck)

The Plot

Lewis was left at an orphanage doorstep as an infant; he was brought inside by Mildred, a kindly woman in charge of the orphanage. Twelve years later, Lewis has had dozens of meetings with prospective adoptive parents but none of them have decided to adopt him, and he has thrown himself into his inventions, much to the annoyance of his young roommate, Michael.

Lewis begins to believe that the only person who ever wanted him was his birth mother, and he works on inventing a memory scanner to help him remember her and then reconnect with her. However, Lewis' presentation at the school science fair is sabotaged by a mysterious villain, but a teenager claiming to be from the future encourages Lewis to repair his invention.

In an attempt to prove to Lewis that he is truly from the future, the teenager, Wilbur, takes Lewis to his home, in the year 2037. There, Lewis is loved by Wilbur's family, the Robinsons, and when they learn that he is an orphan they offer to adopt him; however, when they learn that he is from the past they decide that he cannot stay. He shortly realizes that these are his future parents, wife, children, and extended family. A meeting with his future self inspires him to return to his time and resubmit his science fair invention.

Before returning Lewis to his time, Wilbur keeps an earlier promise and takes Lewis to the moment when Lewis' birth mother left him at the orphanage. Lewis almost greets her but finally opts not to and explains to Wilbur that he did not need to do it, because he already has a family.

Lewis returns to his own time, and shortly after returning he is adopted by a science fair judge and her zany husband, who decides that Lewis should go by the name Cornelius.

The Adoption Connection

After he is disappointed by 124 unsuccessful interviews with prospective adoptive parents, Lewis declares that he will not be rejected again and he becomes driven by a new desire to find his birth mother. When a time-travelling teen from the future inadvertently assures Lewis that he will have a family one day, Lewis decides not to interfere with his birth mother.

He chooses not to change his past and instead chooses to embrace his future.

The mysterious villain who sabotages Lewis' invention is the adult version of Lewis' roommate Michael. He holds a grudge against Lewis because he believes that Lewis' late nights of inventing indirectly prevented him from being adopted. Michael was so tired from sleepless nights sharing a room with Lewis that he missed a key catch in a baseball game, and he was left embittered. Understanding this, Lewis makes use of time travel to help Michael make that catch, which enables Michael to become a joyful kid, and he is eventually adopted.

Strong Points

It is uplifting to see the hope that Lewis takes from knowing that, in the future, he will have a family. It is also fun and fanciful to imagine visiting one's family at different points in time.

Lewis is a kind boy who even reaches out to the villain who has been sabotaging him once he understands the pain that is driving the villain.

It isn't commented on, but it is a time-travelling version of Lewis himself who knocks on the orphanage door to start his journey towards the future; he knocks on the door instead of tapping his birth mother on the shoulder.

Challenges

Mildred heavily coaches Lewis prior to his meeting with a set of prospective adoptive parents; this and other scenes portray a world in which a child has to more or less earn their adoption. After the interview goes poorly, Lewis overhears the infuriated prospective adoptive parents declare that Lewis would not be a good fit for their family. Lewis reacts by declaring that he is almost a teenager, at which point it will be even harder to be adopted, and reaches the conclusion that nobody has ever wanted him, including his birth mother.

When Mildred suggests that his birth mother might have placed him because she was unable to care for him, Lewis changes his mind and believes that his birth mother is the one person in the world who has ever wanted him. The next chapter of life is driven by a desire to remember and find her.

Lewis' decision not to reach out to his birth mother is justified by his belief that he already has a family. Lewis is able to accept his future joyfully, and he decides not to change his past. However, it could be possible for some viewers to believe that his decision not to connect with his birth mother occurs because his adoptive family has replaced his birth mother. It would be unfortunate if viewers finished this film believing that the sign of a healthy adoption is that the adoptee does not need to know their birth parent. That's not the decision Lewis made; he simply chose not to alter his past, and parents might need to help their kids catch that nuance.

Michael became a villain because no one adopted him, and no one adopted him because he was bitter. It is sad to hear that he stayed in the orphanage, alone, even after the orphanage went out of operation. It would be possible for kids watching the movie to believe that it was Michael's fault that he was not adopted and to believe that he became a villain because he was not adopted.

In one scene, Lewis' future family has been brainwashed and try to attack him.

Recommendations

Meet the Robinsons shows the importance of hope for Lewis and also captures the fact that his adoptive family fills the need he feels for a family. Some scenes—including a scene of an infant Lewis being left at the orphanage doorstep on a rainy night, scenes of unsuccessful adoption interviews, and Lewis' decision ultimately to decide against meeting his birth mother—might be hard for some viewers.

This one seems best geared for kids of ages 10–14; after watching it, explore some of the questions below with your kids.

Questions for Discussion

- What would you do if you could travel back in time to when you were a baby? What would you tell your birth parents?

- What would it be like if, like Wilbur, you could see your parents when they were kids?

- Why didn't Lewis tap his birth mother on her shoulder? Would you have done it?

- Lewis is called Cornelius by his new family; how many different names and nicknames have you been called?

- What do you remember about the time before you were adopted?

- If you could go back in time and tell a younger you about today, what would you say? If you could travel to the future, what would you ask grown-up you?

The Odd Life of Timothy Green

(2012, PG, 104 minutes. Live Action. Starring
Jennifer Garner, Joel Edgerton, and CJ Adams)

The Plot

James and Cynthia Green are being interviewed as part
of the process of becoming adoptive parents. Their social
worker wants to get to know them, but reminds them that
they have only a limited time to share their story. Aware
of this, James and Cynthia dive into the remarkable story of
their short time with their son, Timothy.

The Greens remember sitting across from their
fertility doctor and hearing the painful news that although
they've done everything they could have done, they will
not be able to become parents. This news sends them into
a time of great sadness.

Eventually, James and Cynthia spend one evening
daydreaming about what their child would have been like—
loving, brave, and honest. Together, they write out their
dreams on pieces of paper and then bury those papers in the
yard. They believe they've closed this chapter of their life,
and are resigned to childlessness, but a magical storm causes
a child to grow in the ground from the dreams they'd written
down. Timothy is everything they hoped for—loving, brave,
and honest. He also has leaves growing out of his shins. The
Greens weren't expecting that.

The Greens tell Timothy to keep his leaves secret because
people will not understand that he is different. For a while,
he keeps a secret from his parents—that he can only stay
for a little while. Eventually, Timothy leaves, and the Greens
decide to pursue adoption.

The Adoption Connection

James and Cynthia have struggled through years of infertility treatments, as have many who eventually pursue parenthood through adoption.

Timothy comes to the Greens in an unusual way and the Greens try to keep this a secret; this is similar to how some adoptive families feel tempted to shroud their adoption in secrecy. The Greens hope to protect Timothy from others' judgment, and to protect themselves as well, but the secrecy is not healthy or helpful.

Strong Points

James and Cynthia are grieved by the finality of their infertility, but they face their grief head-on, and process it in a unique and creative way; in doing that, they are freed to move on into another stage of their life—and another road to parenthood.

Challenges

The Greens are fearful that the people in their family and community will not understand the unique way in which Timothy came to them. In order to protect him and themselves from derision and judgment, they tell Timothy to keep his origins a secret. He does for a season, but eventually finds it very freeing to let a friend into his secret—and he finds that she has a secret too. It's evident, too, that Timothy was never bothered by his uniqueness; he only kept it secret because of his parents' discomfort. His parents eventually understand this and acknowledge that the reason they kept secrets is because they felt fear and shame.

Unfortunately, the Greens' fears of judgment are not completely unfounded. Cynthia's sister is very condescending and makes a comment suggesting that it's not safe or wise to raise a child who isn't born to you. It's important to note, though, that Cynthia's sister seems likely to say similarly degrading things regardless of the circumstances. Adoption is not the issue; it's the sister's pride.

Timothy's departure from the Greens is rather sudden.

Recommendations

The Odd Life of Timothy Green could be helpful to adults pursuing adoption. It shines in its early moments as James and Cynthia process their infertility together and could provide a model for other adults in a similar situation. It also offers a helpful exploration of the motivations behind secrecy in adoptive families.

Questions for Discussion

- If infertility has been part of your journey to adoption, how have you dealt with your feelings about it? Have they been feelings of loss, or are they more feelings of sadness, envy, or anger? What do you imagine a child born to you would have been like?

- The Greens encourage Timothy to keep his story to himself because people "might not understand." That's an example of Secrecy. How would they have approached it if they were using Confidentiality rather than Secrecy?

- How much pressure do you feel to create a perfect childhood for your child? Is it realistic and reasonable? Is it better to provide a childhood free of sadness or to help a child learn to deal with sadness? Why?

Planes

(2013, PG, 92 minutes. Live Action. Starring
Dane Cook and Stacy Keach)

The Plot

A simple country crop duster plane has dreams of becoming a world-famous racer. He wants to be more than just the farm equipment he was created to be. Dusty Crophopper's dreams of glory are initially ridiculed by those around him; however, with the support of a few friends, Dusty qualifies for a major race. Then, his community comes around him to offer help, training, and support.

The race introduces Dusty to a worldwide audience—and to planes from all over the world. During the race, Dusty wins friends and makes fans through his kindness, but raises the ire of the champion, Ripslinger. The champ attempts to have Dusty knocked out of the race, but Dusty perseveres.

Along the way, Dusty learns that his coach, a navy plane named Skipper, has been exaggerating his war stories; Dusty has to decide whether to trust him still. He does trust him once Skipper explains the truth of his military service.

The Adoption Connection

Although apparently not related to Dusty, Skipper fills a fatherly or grandfatherly role for him.

After leaving his hometown, Dusty sees the world.

One character makes an offhand joke about being separated from a sibling at birth.

Strong Points

Dusty is supported by a loyal, encouraging group of friends.

Dusty is a fine role model and exhibits excellent care and sportsmanship, even saving the life of one of his opponents.

Challenges

Dusty learns that Skipper has lied about his extensive military service; in truth, he only flew one mission, and on that mission he experienced the traumatic losses of his fellow planes. It's surprisingly hard to hear Skipper's painful story, and Dusty's initial response is cold—he would not have asked Skipper to mentor him had he known the truth. However, in telling the truth, Skipper is finally able to process the guilt and shame he feels and is finally able to fly again.

Recommendations

Planes is not an adoption story, but it is a fun, kid-friendly film with bright colors and smiling vehicles that will appeal to viewers of ages 3–10 or so.

Dusty is a good role model, and his story is simple but happy. A side storyline involving Dusty's mentor shows the pain that can be caused by shame and Secrecy and the healing that can occur when Secrecy is broken.

This film could be particularly helpful to kids of ages 6–10 who need help moving away from Secrecy about painful parts of their story; they can enjoy Dusty's unlikely triumphs while also being introduced, through Skipper, to the notion that sharing your secrets with a trustworthy person can help you find healing and feel better.

Questions for Discussion

- Why did Skipper keep his secret for so long? How did Skipper's secret hurt him?

- Skipper was able to fly again after he told the truth about his wartime experience. Why do you think telling his story helped him to feel better?

- Have you ever been betrayed by a friend? By an adult?

Planes: Fire and Rescue

(2014, PG, 84 minutes. Animated. Starring
Dane Cook and Stacy Keach)

The Plot

After his unlikely rise to the top of the racing world, former rural crop duster Dusty Crophopper has become a world-famous celebrity. He is preparing to perform at a local fair, but learns that his internal gear box is failing—if he keeps racing, he will crash. Dusty's friend and mechanic has installed a warning light that will warn him when his system is being dangerously overtaxed.

Dusty tries to find new purpose as a fire and rescue vehicle. He travels to a forest park where he will be trained by Blade, a former entertainer who has also found a second life as a rescue vehicle. The learning process is hard for Dusty. He contemplates walking away, but the typically harsh Blade softens and reminds him that he will not be able to save lives if he walks away.

Dusty does stay and is instrumental in saving the lives of two of his friends.

The Adoption Connection

Dusty has moved from one environment and group of friends into another family-like group. Like *Planes*, this one doesn't have anything directly about adoption, but it could still be helpful to adoptive families who want to talk to their kids about understanding and managing emotions or for families whose kids worry that adoption was a "second choice."

Strong Points

Dusty is brave and driven. When he learns that he cannot continue racing, instead of perseverating on a lost dream, he seeks out and attains a new dream, and it's an altruistic one.

Challenges

Scenes of peril—including scenes involving fire—could be difficult for children who have experienced chaos and trauma prior to coming to their adoptive or foster family.

Recommendations

Kids of ages 3–9 who liked the first *Planes* movie might enjoy this movie.

Adoptive and foster families might value the tachometer that is created for Dusty: it's a dial with a warning light that shows when his internal stress is getting too high, and the hope is that he'll heed its warnings and avoid crashing.

Many kids—and perhaps especially kids who have come from rough places—struggle to understand and manage their emotions. Parents could draw a parallel between Dusty's internal torque and a child's internal feelings. Just like Dusty can know before he crashes, a kid can learn to know when they're starting to get over-tense inside, and they can avoid crashes, too.

This is a good film for most kids of ages 3–9. The film also has applicability to parents whose kids feel that adoption was a "second choice" for their parents. Even though Dusty wanted to be a rescue worker after he had wanted to be a racer, he did not want it less. It's second in sequence rather than second in degree of wanting.

Questions for Discussion

- Can you tell, ahead of time, when your emotions are starting to get very strong? What could help you calm down if you realize this?

- Being a rescue vehicle is Dusty's second dream— earlier, he wanted to be a racer. What do you think it feels like to have a second dream? Did Dusty want the second dream less than he wanted the first one, or is it second only because he wanted it after he had wanted the first one? This could be a helpful analogy for parents who pursued adoption after dealing with infertility, who want to convey the message, "We wanted adoption sequentially after we wanted fertility treatments, but we don't want you less than we wanted a biologically related child."

Family Activity

Use a paper plate and a paper arrow to make a "feeling tachometer" and invite your child to use it regularly to indicate how they're feeling.

Tangled

(2010, PG, 100 minutes. Animated. Starring Mandy
Moore, Zachary Levi, and Donna Murphy)

The Plot

A witch named Gothel has lived for hundreds of years, renewing her youth by harvesting the power of a secret flower. One day, when the pregnant Queen is very ill, some of her subjects discover the flower and use it to bring the Queen back to health. Rapunzel is born, imbued with the power of the flower. Gothel sneaks into the infant's room and tries to cut her hair to harvest the youth-bringing power. When that fails, Gothel steals the infant.

Years later, Rapunzel is a teenager, locked in Gothel's tower. She believes that Gothel is her mother, and that she is kept in the tower for her own safety from the dangerous world outside.

Each year on her birthday, Rapunzel wonders at the floating lights that she sees in the distance and longs to go and see them up close. The lights she sees are lanterns that her parents and their subjects launch in her memory.

One day, when Gothel is away, a runaway thief enters Rapunzel's tower and she convinces him to take her to see the lights. Gothel tries to recapture Rapunzel, but Gothel is killed, which frees Rapunzel to rejoin her parents, who welcome her with profound gladness.

The Adoption Connection

Rapunzel is raised by Gothel and believes that Gothel is the only mother that she ever had. Rapunzel's parents have never forgotten her. This story mirrors a very unfortunate understanding of adoption as kidnapping that is held by some people who have unhealed wounds that they blame on adoption.

It is positive to note that Rapunzel's parents never forgot her; some children wonder if their birth parents forget about them, and *Tangled* suggests that they do not. Parents will need to make sure that their children understand the difference between a legitimate adoption and the circumstance that Gothel has created.

Even though Gothel tries to hide Rapunzel's past, Rapunzel remembers little pieces of it—the truth strives to come out.

Flynn Rider, the runaway thief who takes Rapunzel to the floating lights, acknowledges that he was raised in an orphanage.

Rapunzel explores the town she was born in, though she does not realize it at the time.

Strong Points

Rapunzel has some memories of her life before Gothel, and her parents always remember her. It's important for adopted people to know that their memories are valuable and valid, and to know that they themselves are not forgotten.

The love that Rapunzel's parents have for her is evident in their reunification.

Challenges

Gothel is a master manipulator. Parents could use Gothel as an example to help their children understand when someone is trying to manipulate them, and to point out that people who love them should not try to manipulate them in this way.

The theme of a kidnapper posing as a mother probably pushes this film out of bounds for many adoptive families with young children. When Rapunzel understands what has happened she challenges the right of Gothel to be called "Mother." Gothel responds wickedly, but is killed.

Recommendations

Although it's an animated film, *Tangled* is probably best suited to teenagers and their parents. Younger children might be easily confused by the kidnapper Gothel posing as a parent.

Teenagers might be able to benefit from discussion of manipulation and might also be able to both understand and process the distinction between legitimate adoptions and illegitimate kidnapping. Understanding this distinction could be helpful to your teenagers if they are ever confronted by people who misunderstand adoption or if they ever hear the allegations of people who oppose adoption. Hearing about these allegations first, with you and under your moderation, might help them navigate them more successfully if and when they hear them outside of your home.

Tangled could be used with kids of ages 14–18 or so, but parents should screen it first.

Questions for Discussion

- How did Gothel try to use her words to control Rapunzel's feelings?

- What do you remember from your childhood?

- Why wasn't Gothel an adoptive parent?

Tarzan

(1999, G, 88 minutes. Animated. Starring Tony Goldwyn,
Minnie Driver, Glenn Close, and Rosie O'Donnell)

The Plot

When a ship is wrecked off the coast of Africa, a young couple
survives with their infant son. They build a tree house but are
soon killed by a leopard named Sabor. The infant survives
and is rescued by Kala, a female gorilla whose infant was
recently killed by Sabor. Kala names the infant Tarzan and
brings him back to her tribe. Kershak, Kala's mate and the
leader of the tribe, reluctantly allows Tarzan to stay.

Tarzan makes some friends, but does not quite fit in with
his tribe and struggles to keep up. He never suspects that he
is not a gorilla, and the other gorillas merely make fun of
him for not having fur. Kershak and Kala know that he is a
human but have not told him. Tarzan does wonder why his
hands do not look like Kala's; she tells him to focus on the
fact that their hearts beat the same.

One day, Tarzan meets humans who have come to
the jungle to explore. His first encounter is with a kind
young woman named Jane and he is astonished to realize
that her hands look like his. Tarzan is fascinated by Jane,
her father Professor Porter, and their guide Clayton.
Kershak forbids Tarzan to continue seeing the humans, but
Tarzan keeps going.

Clayton is untrustworthy and attempts to use Tarzan to
lead him to the gorillas; he hopes to capture them. Tarzan
realizes this and fights Clayton off, but Clayton and Kershak
both die as a result of the battle. With his dying breath,
Kershak finally accepts Tarzan and appoints him leader of
the tribe. Tarzan had planned to leave the tribe to live with

Jane and Professor Porter; now he chooses to stay, and the tribe gladly accepts Jane and Professor Porter as members.

The Adoption Connection

Tarzan has been adopted by Kala. Although he questions whether he belongs in the tribe or why he does not look like her, she assures him that he belongs with her. She eventually tells him about his human parents and shares his baby pictures with him. When Tarzan considers leaving to live with humans, Kala expresses her love for him and assures him that she wants him to be happy regardless of whether he stays with the gorillas or leaves; Tarzan assures her that she is truly his mother.

Strong Points

Lori Holden (Holden and Hass, 2013) writes that it is healthiest for adoptive families to think of their children as being part of both their adoptive family and their birth family, rather than being part of only one or the other.

In Disney's 1967 film *The Jungle Book*, the human child Mowgli is pushed by his jungle family to return to a human town—seemingly suggesting that he must be part of one community and cannot be part of the other. Three decades after *The Jungle Book*, Disney released this story of a boy being raised by animals in the jungle; this time they allow Tarzan to be both a human and a proud child of gorillas.

Kala is a very nurturing mother and immediately takes a liking to Tarzan.

Although his reluctance is troubling, Kershak does wisely caution Kala that Tarzan will not replace the son they lost. She agrees with this, but still wants to adopt Tarzan because she wants to meet his needs.

Kershak ultimately asks Tarzan for forgiveness for his lack of understanding and affirms that Tarzan has always been part of the family.

Challenges

The violence implied in the deaths of Tarzan's parents might be hard for some young viewers, as might the just-slightly-off-camera death by hanging of a villain.

Tarzan's tribe, and Kala's husband in particular, are quite reluctant to accept him. Comments are made that suggest that Tarzan does not belong with the gorillas because he is not a gorilla; younger characters mock his looks. Although he later recants, Kershak hurtfully says that Tarzan is not his son and that he will never be one of the family.

It probably will not bother most young viewers, but some might view Tarzan as partially responsible for Kershak's death. Kershak is killed by Clayton, who only encounters Kershak because Tarzan disobeys Kershak's order to not bring the humans to the gorilla home. Tarzan apologizes to Kershak as Kershak is dying, but Kershak says that Tarzan doesn't need to apologize—that Kershak himself owes Tarzan an apology.

Recommendations

Tarzan struggles to fit in with his new family, but is loved deeply by his mother. He learns about his human heritage and decides to embrace both of his worlds.

This film seems best geared to kids of ages 7 and up. It could be particularly helpful for families that have adopted cross-culturally; one of the film's theme songs reflects on one family being formed from people from different places. This film could be helpful for starting discussions about belonging to two different families or as a safe way to help a child talk about feeling as though sometimes they don't fit in.

Questions for Discussion

- By the end of the movie, was Tarzan part of a human family, a gorilla family, or both at the same time?

- Which do you think was worse for Tarzan: when his friends made fun of him or when Kershak said he wasn't going to become one of the tribe?

- Did Kershak apologizing at the end take away the pain that Tarzan had felt before?

- What things do you think might help Tarzan feel like part of the gorilla family?

- What do you think it's like to be from two different families at the same time?

Tarzan 2

(2005, G, 74 minutes. Animated. Starring Harrison Chad,
Glenn Close, George Carlin, and Estelle Harris)

The Plot

The human boy Tarzan was adopted as an infant by the gorilla, Kala. The first Tarzan movie shows his infancy and adulthood; *Tarzan 2* is an interquel that shows him as a young boy.

Kala is loving and nurturing towards Tarzan, even though her mate Kershak has been resistant to having Tarzan in the family and in spite of the second-guessing by the other females in her tribe. Tarzan struggles to keep up with the other youngsters and fears that one day he will be caught by the Zugor, a monster who is rumored to live nearby.

One day, an accident leads Kala to believe that Tarzan has died. Tarzan manages to make it back to his tribe, but before he rejoins them, he overhears some of the mothers in the tribe saying that it is better without Tarzan. Heartbroken and hurt, Tarzan runs away, vowing to leave the tribe behind for the tribe's own good.

While on the run, Tarzan encounters an old gorilla. Over time, they become friends, and Tarzan asks the old one to help him learn who he is, since he does not appear to be a gorilla.

In the meantime, two of Tarzan's best friends have come to believe that Tarzan is still alive. They set off to find him, and soon Kala also learns that Tarzan might still be alive. Tarzan is initially found by his friends and refuses to go home with them. When his mother Kala arrives, she falls into peril. Tarzan saves her, realizes that his identity is uniquely his own, and affirms that he is part of her family. Together, Tarzan, Kala, and his friends go back to the tribe.

The Adoption Connection

Tarzan has been adopted by a family of gorillas. Issues of identity are present in both this film and the first film in the series. Here, Tarzan is appreciated by some of his peers but not fully accepted, and he questions his identity. Tarzan runs away, and says he will not return until he gets good at being an ape. While away from home, Tarzan tries to figure out his identity and wonders if he might not even have an identity. Eventually, Tarzan learns who he is; although he is not physically a gorilla, he belongs to the family, and his own uniqueness can be a strength rather than a liability.

At one point, Tarzan has a dream of losing his mother.

A song that plays at different points in the film refers to people from two worlds coming together to form one family.

Strong Points

Tarzan is, at times, able to tell Kala that he is feeling as though he doesn't fit in, and she responds wonderfully, affirming that his family needs him and assuring him that his differences do not stop him from fitting in.

Kala's love for Tarzan and grief at his disappearance is immediate and obvious; kids will be able to see that Tarzan's mother deeply loves and misses him, even though Tarzan thought the tribe would be better without him.

Challenges

Tarzan is mocked by his peers for not fitting in but is even more hurt by what he overhears from his mother's friends—that she's better off without Tarzan.

Villains destroy the Zugor's home in one scene, which could trigger some kids who have experienced violence prior to coming to your home.

Recommendations

Tarzan 2 seems most likely to appeal to kids of ages 4–9.

Because Tarzan struggles with both acceptance by others and self-acceptance, this might be a particularly helpful film for kids who have struggled to feel as though they fit in to their new family.

Kids adopted cross-culturally might find it helpful to have an animated young hero who also struggles with these feelings. Parents would want to make sure to point out that kids do not need to run away (Tarzan does eventually apologize for running away). Parents would also want to affirm that the gorillas speaking unkindly about Tarzan were wrong.

Questions for Discussion

- What made it hard for Tarzan to feel as though he fit in with his family? What feelings do you think he had? What could have helped?

- Have you ever overheard someone say something about you that hurt your feelings?

- Do you ever have dreams about your life before we became a family?

- Why did Tarzan run away from his tribe? What could he have done instead? What could his mother have done to make it less likely that he would feel the need to run away?

- What is Tarzan: A gorilla? A human? A Tarzan? A Zugor? What makes him who he is?

- Who are you? What makes you who you are?

- What was it like for Tarzan to be part of a family that didn't look like him?

- Can you be more than one thing at once?

The Tigger Movie

(2000, G, 77 minutes. Animated. Starring Jim
Cummings, Nikita Hopkins, and Peter Cullen)

The Plot

After he becomes sad that his friends cannot bounce as he can, Tigger is inspired to look for a family of other Tiggers; after all, he is the only Tigger in the Hundred Acre Wood, but he believes that there must be some more Tiggers out there.

Tigger misunderstands the concept of a family tree and sets off to find a literal tree that houses other Tiggers. When he fails to find this, his friends decide to write him a letter and sign it as his family. Tigger misunderstands this and believes that the Tiggers to whom he is related will visit him the next day.

His friends try to dress up as Tiggers rather than telling him that he has misinterpreted their letter, but Tigger sees through their disguises and storms out, upset. His friends follow after him and find him alone. Although he initially refuses to go back with them, an avalanche requires him to rescue most of his friends, and one of his friends rescues him with a particularly Tigger-like move. Tigger then learns that his friends wrote the letter, and he comes to an understanding that his friends are his family.

The Adoption Connection

Roo comments that, since Roo has parents, there must be other Tiggers in the world since Tigger must have parents too. This leads our familiar bouncy Tigger optimistically to hope to find them. He had previously been feeling lonely after noticing that he is the only Tigger he knows, but now he sings joyfully about the hope of finding family that looks and acts like he does. Tigger tries to find his family by writing a letter and then by taking a journey, but he does not find them and feels disappointed.

His friends try to pretend to be Tiggers by dressing up and talking like him, but this only hurts Tigger's feelings. He does embrace them as family when he realizes that they love him and that he loves them. Roo wants Tigger to be his brother, and Tigger eventually expresses that he considers Roo a brother.

Tigger is excited to find a locket, believing that it will contain pictures of his family. He is saddened to find it empty, but later fills it with a picture of himself with his friends.

Strong Points

Although some of their efforts are misguided, the love that Tigger's friends have for him is obvious: Owl encourages him to look for his family, Roo accompanies him on his search, most of his friends try different ways to lift his spirits, and all of his friends look for him when he storms away.

The Tigger Movie captures and deals with the difficult fact that not every search for birth family members will result in finding them. Tigger is consoled by realizing that his friends have become his family, and that because of them, he is not alone.

The movie also shows that a person can miss their birth family, even if they have no memory of meeting them. Kanga makes a comment that suggests that it would be normal for Tigger to feel that way sometimes.

Kanga tells Roo that Tigger will always be a part of their family because they care about him.

Challenges

Tigger sings sadly about being the loneliest person, and he ties this into the fact that he does not know anyone who looks or acts like him. While some young viewers might find this to be a very sad song, it can communicate to parents that it can be important for kids adopted cross-culturally or adopted into multiethnic or multiracial families to have access to people who look like them and access to their cultures of origin.

One character suggests that the friends should not help Tigger look for other Tiggers, exasperatedly adding that one is enough.

Tigger's friends mean well, but they are somewhat dishonest with him, and when he realizes it, he is so angry that he decides to leave his friends in search of what he imagines will be his truest family.

Rabbit tells Tigger that it is silly to look for other Tiggers, and that Tigger should give up. Tigger forcefully refuses Rabbit's advice.

Recommendations

The Tigger Movie seems best geared to viewers of ages 4–8 and their parents, although the topics in the film could be helpful to older viewers as well.

After watching this with your kids, consider inviting them to share what they feel, think, wish, and imagine about their birth family. You can validate their feelings of longing and their feelings of belonging with you; both sets of feelings can exist at the same time!

Questions for Discussion

- In what ways are you like your family? In what ways are you distinct from them?

- Why did Tigger want to find other Tiggers? What did he want to do with them?

- When he started his search, how important did Tigger think it was to know family members that look like him? How important would it be for you, if you were Tigger?

- Why did Tigger's friends try to dress up like Tigger? Why did it make Tigger sad? Do you think they should have done that? If not, what could they have done instead?

- Who do you imagine you get your looks from? What do you get from your adoptive family?

- If you had a locket, and could put a picture of anyone you wanted inside, who would be in it? What if you could fit three or four pictures inside? (There can be more than one person in each picture!)

- Do you ever miss your birth family? If you could write them a letter, what would it say? If you could receive a letter from them, what do you hope it would say?

- Tigger was disappointed more than once in this movie. What helped him recover from the disappointment?

- Tigger receives a letter, and decides in his mind that it means that his family will come to see him tomorrow. Why do you think he started thinking that? Would it have been kind or unkind for his friends to tell him that he was wrong?

• Have you ever felt like Tigger?

Family Activity

Find a picture locket or a small wallet or photo album and pictures of the people that your child names in response to the question earlier in this review. Help them put the pictures into the locket, wallet, or album. Your child might find it meaningful or comforting to be able to carry these pictures with them, whenever they want!

Up

(2009, PG, 96 minutes. Animated. Starring Ed Asner, Christopher Plummer, and Jordan Nagai)

The Plot

As a young boy, Carl Fredricksen idolized the explorer Charles Muntz, who exiled himself to Paradise Falls in order to bring back a bird that he had reported discovering, but which the scientific community doubted. Carl met Ellie, a young girl who also idolized Muntz. They fell in love, grew up together, and married, always planning to take a trip to Paradise Falls.

After their marriage, they traded their dreams of Paradise Falls for dreams of parenthood, but Ellie suffered a miscarriage and learned that she would not be able to deliver a baby. They were heartbroken, but again set their sights on Paradise Falls.

Pressing issues kept preventing their journey, but in their retirement, Carl decided to make the trip happen; unfortunately, Ellie died prior to departing.

Now a stubborn old man, Carl refuses to leave the home that he shared with Ellie. When his home is threatened, he sets it aloft with balloons, deciding at last to go to Paradise Falls. He unintentionally brings a passenger with him—Russell, a young Scout who hoped to earn a merit badge by serving the elderly.

When the house reaches Paradise Falls, Carl faces dilemmas that make him choose between clinging to the past or honoring it while embracing the present.

The Adoption Connection

Carl and Ellie dealt with crushing infertility, as have many families that have pursued adoption. After receiving the news, they set their sights on other dreams. Those dreams go unfulfilled, but they still find happiness in life.

Russell misses his father; his father has become distant from Russell in the wake of his remarriage to a woman who says that Russell talks to his father too much. Russell's father seems to neglect him, even failing to attend an important ceremony, but Carl becomes a stand-in father figure for him.

Strong Points

Carl and Ellie both found ways to go on with life in spite of disappointments. Carl finds that Ellie has kept a scrapbook of her life. She found joy in her life, rather than being consumed by sadness over the joys that she did not experience.

Challenges

The first ten minutes of the film are powerful and can produce tears, which might catch viewers off-guard since this is an animated film. Parents watching it on their own might want to be prepared for the emotions they might feel around infertility and the eventual death of a spouse; parents watching with children might need to be prepared to offer an age-appropriate explanation of infertility and might also have to console children who are sad when Ellie dies.

Recommendations

The first ten minutes or so of *Up* are some of the most powerful minutes ever captured in a movie. The animated characters nearly wordlessly grow from children into young adults, and from young adults into seniors. They deal with infertility and delayed dreams but still find joy in the life they share together before one of them passes away. While *Up* is likely to be viewed as a kids' film, those ten minutes can stand alongside any adult drama.

Up will appeal to kids who will enjoy the colorful floating house and Dug the talking dog, but *Up* is also a good choice for a parents' date night. Kids can be inspired by Russell's bravery. Parents can be challenged and inspired by the way in which Carl continually recreates and redirects his life. This one is good for kids, families, and couples.

Questions for Discussion (for Kids)

- Why does Russell think his dad isn't around anymore? How do you think he feels about it?

- What does Russell think of Carl by the end of the movie?

- What is the nicest thing that Carl does for Russell? What is the nicest thing that Russell does for Carl?

- What do you think it would be like to have a talking dog? If our pet could talk, what do you think it would talk about?

Questions for Discussion (for Parents)

- If you're a couple, what attracted you to each other?

- What dreams have you had that have been fulfilled? Which haven't been?

- If infertility or childlessness has been part of your journey to adoption, how have you dealt with your feelings regarding it?

- Have you ever replaced old dreams with new ones? Do you want the new dreams to a different degree than you wanted the old ones?

- How do you go on with life after facing a huge disappointment? If you have suffered a miscarriage, how do you incorporate that into your life story?

Chapter 6

MORE MOVIES FOR KIDS

Many fond memories can be formed by sharing family movie nights. Here are some movies that can help make those memories of shared entertainment. They also lend themselves to helping start conversations about adoption issues. These movies are mostly geared towards children, and the questions provided are also geared towards children. Some of the questions that follow focus on wanting to be adopted, family and identity development, and sibling relationships. There are also some questions to help your kids talk about their experiences, some fanciful questions for fun, and some suggested activities to do as a family.

The Boxtrolls

(2014, PG, 96 minutes. Animated. Starring Isaac Hempstead-Wright, Elle Fanning, Ben Kingsley, and Tracy Morgan)
Awards: 2015 Adoption at the Movies Awards Best
Adoptive Parent and Best Adoptive Family

The Plot

Ten years ago, the town of Cheesebridge was terrified at the disappearance of Herbert Trubshaw and his infant son.

Archibald Snatcher, a lower-caste pest exterminator, blamed the disappearance on Boxtrolls, subterranean trolls who come out at night to take discarded metal.

Snatcher wants to be included in the ruling class, and obtains the agreement of Lord Portley-Rind that if he exterminates all of the Boxtrolls, he will be granted membership. Each year, Snatcher catches more and more Boxtrolls and the townspeople hold a festival to commemorate the disappearance of the Trubshaw Baby.

In the meantime, a young human boy called Eggs is being raised by the Boxtrolls, and his father figure is a nurturing Boxtroll named Fish. When Fish is captured, Eggs tries to find him and catches the attention of a young girl named Winnie. He explains his story to her and sets off to rescue Fish.

Later, Fish tells him the story of how he came to be with the Boxtrolls: Archibald Snatcher attacked Herbert Trubshaw, and Herbert entrusted his son to the Boxtrolls to keep him safe from Snatcher. Eggs tries to tell the townspeople that he is the missing baby and that the Boxtrolls are not dangerous, but they do not believe him, and Snatcher has almost succeeded in collecting all of the Boxtrolls. He also captures Eggs and holds him as a prisoner next to his father, Herbert.

Snatcher disguises Eggs as a Boxtroll and prepares to kill him publicly as the last remaining Boxtroll, but all of the Boxtrolls have escaped Snatcher's attempt to kill them and return to save Eggs. Snatcher explodes due to an allergic reaction, and the Boxtrolls are able to live at peace with the rest of the community while Eggs and Herbert are reunited.

The Adoption Connection

Eggs has been raised by Fish for ten years and has been given a Boxtroll name. He has never heard the story of how he came to Fish and believes that he is a Boxtroll. When he meets Winnie she challenges this belief, noting that he looks like her rather than like a Boxtroll. Like in *Tarzan*, the theme of their hands looking alike or different is part of her discourse. This leads to Fish telling Eggs the story of how Eggs came to be a part of the Boxtrolls.

By the end of the film, Eggs has been reunified with Herbert and continues to be close to Fish as well; all three of them ride off together at the end of the film.

Strong Points

Fish is a very nurturing parent. When he shares his story with Eggs, it is quite thorough, and Fish affirms that he did not steal Eggs from Eggs' father, but was entrusted with him.

The film has a wonderful definition of what a father is. Some of that is that a father is someone who raises, looks after, and loves their child. Eggs suggests that Fish is like a father to him by that definition.

A song at the end of the film suggests that families can come in different sorts, and that we should be glad for our families and offer love to people without families.

Challenges

In one scene, Fish is pulled away from Eggs' hands by an exterminator; kids could find it traumatic to see a child separated from a parent in this way. Later, Eggs thinks he sees Fish die; this could be very hard for young viewers who have lost parents. Eggs also believes for a season that Herbert has been killed by the exterminators. Although neither Fish nor Herbert die, the scenes could be scary for some kids.

Recommendations

The Boxtrolls seems geared towards older kids, while some younger viewers might be easily bothered by scenes of peril in which parental loss is threatened.

The film's main power for adoptive families seems to be in the definition of a father, and in the scene in which Fish tells Eggs his story. Honesty about adoption is refreshing to see in film, and the film's definition of fatherhood is a positive one focused on kindness, attention, and nurturing.

Questions of identity are also relevant to the film; Eggs' history is provided to him in the context of questions about his identity.

This film seems best suited to kids of ages 10 and up, and perhaps to teens as well. Viewers of this age will likely enjoy the film and benefit from the discussions that the film can invite.

Questions for Discussion

- Snatcher tried to use fear to turn the people against the Boxtrolls, hoping to use that fear to indirectly put himself into a position of privilege. What do you think of that?

- In what ways is Eggs a Boxtroll? Are there any ways in which he is more of a human than a Boxtroll?

- Now that Eggs has both Herbert and Fish, does he have two dads? What do you think that's like?

- If you were a Boxtroll, what would your name be?

- What is a dad?

- If you wrote a song about your family, what would it be called? What would the song say?

Choose Your Own Adventure: The Abominable Snowman

(2006, G, 85 minutes total (a typical story could be around 15 minutes). Animated. Starring William H. Macy and Frankie Muniz)

The Plot

Siblings Benjamin, Crista, and Marco North set off to Nepal to join their Uncle Rudy, who is in search of the mysterious Yeti. The North kids are adventurers, like their late parents. Benjamin is technologically inclined, Crista is athletic, and Marco, who was adopted from Guatemala by the Norths, is very brave.

When the kids' plane has problems, they have to decide whether to parachute out or stay aboard. Actually, the viewer chooses. This film is based on the *Choose Your Own Adventure* books, and viewers are asked occasionally to decide between two options for the characters to take.

There are at least 11 different endings to the film; most are positive, but there are a few negative ones. The best ending sees the kids and Uncle Rudy reunited and able to explore a new paradise; the worst ending—and the only fatal one—has the kids get eaten by a tiger (but the viewer has to make several poor choices for this ending to occur). Every ending is followed by the question "The End?" and viewers are invited to revisit and change any of the choices they made on the journey.

The Adoption Connection

Marco was adopted from Guatemala. He joins his older siblings in following in the footsteps of their late parents. Together, the siblings process their feelings about their parents being gone; their parents died on an adventure, and one child expresses anger at them for making risky choices that led to the children being alone. They also take pride in being adventurous like their parents, and in one outcome they are able to join the same society of adventurers that their parents had once belonged to.

Adoption and parental loss are mentioned in the first four minutes of the film, before any choices are made, but only as background information to the story that is about to unfold.

Strong Points

Young kids might find it particularly fun to influence the outcome of a cartoon.

There is a great sense of family pride in the North clan. Marco's adoption is mentioned and never hidden, but it's also not a major plot point; it's just part of life for the North family.

One character has been hurt by the losses in his life; he is told that he has fear and anger where there should be love, and he is given a choice (the viewer must choose for him) of whether to stay completely safe but alone or to live a life of adventure and risk with those he loves. One of those choices leads to the story's best ending, while the other choice leads to a frustrating ending.

Challenges

Four negative endings might frustrate some kids; only one is particularly scary.

Recommendations

Choose Your Own Adventure: The Abominable Snowman is a fun, interactive movie that will probably appeal most to kids of ages 5–8.

There is a peripheral adoption connection, and all the young characters deal with a previous loss of their parents. They do find a sense of family in each other and in their uncle. Try this one out a few times with your kids. Make your own trails, and see what you discover.

Questions for Discussion

- What adventures have you had in your life? What adventures would you wish to have?

- How do our choices affect our lives?

- Sometimes we get to make choices; other times we only get to choose our responses to other people's choices or to things that happen that no one chose. How do you decide what choices to make? Has there ever been a time when you made a choice without realizing that you made a choice at all?

- The North kids were explorers, like the rest of their family. What parts of you come from your birth family? What parts of you come from your adoptive family? Are there any parts of you that are a combination of both of those?

- Which ending was your favorite?

Curly Top

(1935, G, 74 minutes. Live Action. Starring Shirley
Temple, John Boles, and Rochelle Hudson)

The Plot

Elizabeth Blair has lived in the Lakeside Orphanage since her parents passed away. Her young adult sister, Mary, has managed to stay close to her by working in the orphanage.

When the trustees of the orphanage come to visit, Elizabeth gets into trouble by mimicking one of the senior trustees, who threatens to send her away; she is protected by a wealthy young trustee, Edward Morgan. Edward comes to love Elizabeth, and wishes to adopt her. He has also developed romantic feelings for Mary.

Edward speaks to the orphanage director about his desire to adopt Elizabeth. However, he wants to let Elizabeth be free from the obligation to be effusively thankful for every kindness shown to her, so he attempts to hide his identity from her, telling her instead that a fictional friend named Hiram Jones wishes to adopt her and will accept Mary as well.

Elizabeth and Mary both go to Edward's home, and eventually Edward, Mary, and Elizabeth all realize and communicate their desire to become a family.

The Adoption Connection

Elizabeth and Mary were orphaned when their parents died in a car accident.

The orphanage where Elizabeth and Mary live is run by two ladies; they both care for the girls there, but one of them—the orphanage superintendent Mrs. Higgins—is harsh.

Edward speaks to Elizabeth about providing nice things for her. Elizabeth comments that she thought only parents could do nice things like that for children, and that's when Edward suggests legal adoption as a way for someone else to provide for a child.

Before he commits to adopting Elizabeth, Edward daydreams and sings about having her in his life. In his song, adoptive parents might recognize their own love for, and desire to adopt, a particular child.

Strong Points

The film shows the desire of children—and of parents—to love and be loved.

Mary is a devoted sister to Elizabeth. She promised her parents that she would stay with Elizabeth and has actively maintained that commitment. Elizabeth's dedication to Mary is also very strong.

The matrons of the orphanage note that they always hoped that the girls would be adopted, and they cry tears of joy when Elizabeth and Mary do find a permanent home.

Edward isn't alone in his adoption of Elizabeth; he consults with, and is supported by, his live-in aunt Genevieve, who assures him that she would love to have a child's laughter in the home.

Once her own situation is secure, Elizabeth remembers the other children from her orphanage and tries to help them.

Challenges

Mrs. Higgins is too harsh. She tells Elizabeth that she is a wicked child, suggests that her parents failed at raising her, and threatens to send away Elizabeth's pets because of her behavior. Although these pets were inherited from

Elizabeth's parents, Mrs. Higgins admonishes Elizabeth not to pout about this decision. The senior trustee is also unkind towards Elizabeth and Mary.

Although Edward's intention to let Elizabeth live in childlike happiness is kindhearted, he begins his pursuit of adoption of her on false grounds, not even acknowledging that he is her intended adoptive parent.

Recommendations

Curly Top's Shirley Temple-focused song and dance routines seem most likely to appeal to young children up to age 9 or so, and might be more appealing to girls than boys.

The film highlights the desire of adoptive parents to love the children they care for, and also depicts a strong sibling relationship. Unfortunately, it also captures some of the secrecy that is sometimes present in adoption, but parents could be intentional about challenging Edward's secrecy and affirming their own commitment to honesty about adoption.

Curly Top could be particularly good for siblings who have been adopted together.

Questions for Discussion

- Why did Edward make up Hiram Jones, rather than telling the truth that he wanted to adopt Elizabeth? Do you think he was right or wrong to do this?

- How important was it that Elizabeth and Mary stayed together? Why are sisters and brothers so important to each other?

- Elizabeth sang songs imagining what she might be when she grows up, but even as a kid she tried to help other children who were still in the orphanage. What do you think you'll be when you grow up?

- Were you ever in a place like an orphanage? If not, where did you live before you were adopted? What was it like?

- Mary has felt responsible for Elizabeth, but Elizabeth has also been cared for by the orphanage and by Edward. Have you ever felt responsible for taking care of one of your sisters or brothers? What was that like?

Despicable Me

(PG, 2010, 95 minutes. Animated. Starring Steve Carell, Jason Segal, and Russell Brand)

The Plot

Supervillain Gru needs to steal a shrink ray from a rival, Vector, in order to steal the moon. He is unable to access Vector's base but notices that three young girls, Margo, Edith, and Agnes, are able to enter it easily because they are selling cookies. Gru decides to adopt the girls in order to use their cookie-selling business as a cover for him to steal the shrink ray. He disguises himself and fools the unkind orphanage director Miss Hattie into letting him take the girls home.

Once the girls distract Vector, allowing Gru to steal the shrink ray, Gru tries to abandon them at a county fair. At the fair, though, Gru warms to them and starts to love them. Fearing that this will stop Gru from being an effective villain, Gru's colleague Dr. Nefario calls Miss Hattie and tells her that Gru wishes to return the girls. Miss Hattie picks the girls up and shames them for being returned.

Gru is grieved at losing the girls, and ultimately decides to rejoin them, but learns that they have been kidnapped by Vector. Gru must save the girls and convince them that he will never betray them again.

The Adoption Connection

Gru does eventually adopt the girls and becomes a family with them.

Strong Points

Gru does finally come to love the girls. They start to warm up to him once he sticks up for them. Later, after he appears to have abandoned them, he has to convince Margo that he will never leave her again. Gru's apology is genuine.

Gru puts his repentance into a story and uses that as a bedtime story for the girls once they've rejoined him.

Challenges

Miss Hattie is cruel. Although Margo, Edith, and Agnes want to be adopted, she tells them that it will never happen for them. She uses the children in her charge for free labor. Her punishments involve having the girls sit in a cardboard box called the Box of Shame, which is emotional abuse.

Gru's initial motivations for adopting the girls were selfish and sinister. Although he eventually comes to love them, Miss Hattie should have noticed some of the many concerning factors about him. Kids might need to be told the difference between the way adoptions work in the real world and how it worked for Gru.

While it can be helpful for children to know a home's rules early on, Gru's rules are bad: kids are banned from laughing and crying, among other things. Gru is unprepared to be a parent and has set out food and newspaper on the floor for the girls, as though they are dogs.

Gru tries to abandon the girls.

Recommendations

Despicable Me is a funny and fast-paced movie that will probably naturally appeal to most kids and might be best for kids of ages 8–12.

Some kids, and perhaps especially younger kids, might have a hard time with the concept of the girls being given back to the orphanage. Some kids might be understandably bothered by Gru's unsavory initial motivations for bringing the girls into his home.

For other viewers, this movie could be a helpful picture of how broken relationships can be restored and how parents sometimes need to apologize. The story Gru writes for the girls at the end effectively communicates his new understanding of parental love in a language the girls understand and could be used to inspire your family to create a family storybook as well. Parents would want to affirm that they would never give their kids back.

Questions for Discussion

- How do you think people who want to adopt become adoptive parents? How do you think that people who want to adopt can prove that they are safe?

- What needed to happen for the girls to be able to trust Gru again after they had to go back to Miss Hattie's place? What do you think of that?

- If there was a story based on our family, what would it be called? What would the characters be?

- Has a grown-up ever apologized to you? How did it feel when they did that?

Family Activity

Together, write and illustrate the family story that your kid dreamed up in response to the question in this review!

Despicable Me 2

(2013, PG, 98 minutes. Animated. Starring Steve Carell, Kristen Wiig, and Russell Brand)

The Plot

Former supervillain Gru has settled down into life as a single adoptive dad to Margo, Edith, and Agnes. Agnes is preparing for a Mother's Day presentation at school; as she practices, she emotionlessly recites a poem about mothers and expresses that she often thinks about having a mother.

Meanwhile, the Anti-Villain League has sent the upbeat agent Lucy Wilde to bring Gru in; they hope that he will help them discover which villain has committed the recent theft of a mutagen.

While working side by side with Lucy, Gru starts to fall in love with her. Agnes teases Gru about it while also wishing that Lucy would become her mother. After foiling the villainous El Macho, Gru and Lucy do get married, and Margo, Edith, and Agnes gain a mom.

The Adoption Connection

Gru has adopted Margo, Edith, and Agnes and has gone from being a prickly villain to a nurturing father; early in the film, he dresses as a fairy princess for Agnes' party when a hired performer fails to show up.

Although they are happy with Gru, Agnes particularly wishes for a mother and is able to express that wish to some extent.

Strong Points

Gru has become a very good and loving dad; he is doting towards Agnes at her party and very protective of Margo when she meets her first boyfriend. It's charming to see how Gru has come to love his kids and how they have come to love him.

The film shares the joy that Gru and his kids feel when Lucy joins their family.

Challenges

Gru's longtime assistant temporarily abandons him and helps in the kidnapping and reprogramming of some of Gru's loveable yellow Minions. He eventually realizes the error of his ways and reverses his villainous work, but some kids might be scared by the concept of kidnapping.

Recommendations

Despicable Me 2 is a fun movie that balances tender moments between Gru and his kids, the action and mystery of a supervillain/spy movie, and the frenetic energy of the Minions.

It seems to be a good fit for most families touched by adoption. It can serve to normalize adoption and give kids adopted characters to relate to. While many films feature the formation of an adoptive family, in *Despicable Me 2*, the adoption is already established and the family is thriving.

Despicable Me 2 might be particularly useful for single-parent families who want to give their kids a chance to talk about how they feel about being in a single-parent home.

Despicable Me 2 does not include the parental abandonment and adoption disruption of the first film, which lets its appeal stretch to include younger kids as well as my recommended age group for the first movie. This film seems most likely to appeal to kids of ages 3–12.

Questions for Discussion

- Are there any holidays that are hard for you that aren't hard for some other people?

- How do you feel about the way our family is made up? Do you ever wish that there were more people in it?

- What makes Gru a cool dad? What do you imagine the family will be like now that Lucy is the girls' mom?

- (For single-parent homes) Agnes wished for a mom and also really loved her dad, Gru. Do you ever think about what it would be like to have a second parent in the home? What would you hope for if I got married? What do you like best about our family the way it is now?

Earth to Echo

(2014, PG, 89 minutes. Live Action. Starring Teo Halm, Brian
"Astro" Bradley, Reese C. Hartwig, and Ella Wahlestedt)

The Plot

The neighborhood of Mulberry Woods is being uprooted by
a construction project. Young teenage friends Tuck, Alex, and
Munch get together for one last night of friendship before
they all have to move away. They spend the night following
mysterious displays on their cellphones, which lead them to
Echo, a small alien whose ship has crash-landed.

Echo leads them and their new friend, Emma, on a hunt
for pieces required to repair his ship. The friends help Echo
and, in doing so, save their neighborhood.

Two of the boys still move away, but they continue to
keep in touch as friends; after all, one says, if we have a friend
in outer space, we can certainly maintain these friendships
even after we don't all live in the same town.

The Adoption Connection

Alex is a foster child. Everyone is packing up their belongings
to leave Mulberry Woods, but one of Alex's friends mentions
that Alex has never really unpacked and that all of Alex's
belongings fit in one bag. Kids who have been moved from
one home to another might resonate with the film's themes
of being uprooted and worrying about losing friendships
because of moving.

Alex feels as though he has been abandoned in the past
and this has affected him in two ways: he is fearful and
sensitive to being abandoned again, and he is very loyal to
friends, being careful not to abandon them.

The characters begin to empathize with the alien when they realize that he just wants to go home.

Strong Points

Alex is an example of a brave and loyal teen in foster care. He teaches the distressed alien how to use self-soothing techniques and advocates strongly against abandoning him. Alex explains that he remembers what it feels like to be left, and so he won't leave anyone else.

Alex feels abandoned by one of his friends. They fight briefly, but then the friend understands what happened and manages to repair the relationship.

The film affirms that friendships can be maintained even over great distance, which could be a comforting thought for kids who have been placed in foster or adoptive homes at a distance from the neighborhoods in which they grew up.

Challenges

Parents tend to be clueless, and the teens do run away for a night. They also commit an act of burglary.

One character asks Alex why his foster parents need him, since they already have a baby.

Recommendations

The film's positive message is that friendships can be maintained over distance; this could also be used to affirm that relationships between siblings or other relatives can also be maintained over distance, which could be helpful for kids who have been adopted separately from their siblings.

This seems like a good fit for kids of ages 8–12.

Questions for Discussion

- Do you think Alex, Tuck, and Munch will be able to stay friends even after they move? What will help them do that? What could their parents do to help?

- Why do you think Alex had not unpacked his room?

- Why was Alex so mad when he felt abandoned?

- How did Echo feel when the boys found him?

- If you met an alien, what questions would you ask it? Would you help it?

Ernest and Celestine

(2012, PG, 79 minutes. Animated. Originally
in French; English-dubbed version starring
Forest Whitaker and Mackenzie Foy)

The Plot

Bears live above ground, and mice live below ground. They fear each other. Mice believe that bears will eat them; bears have an innate fear of mice. The mice wouldn't have anything to do with bears except that they need the bears' baby teeth to practice dentistry; after all, without good strong teeth, mice can't gnaw. Young mice are required to sneak above ground to take bear cubs' baby teeth from under their pillow.

One night, an artistic young mouse named Celestine is spotted by a bear family and trapped in a garbage can. She is discovered by a starving musical bear named Ernest. Ernest initially tries to eat her, but Celestine protests and instead tells him where he can find a wealth of sweets.

Overjoyed at his bounty, Ernest becomes friends with Celestine. He eventually helps her steal a sizable collection of old bear teeth, but in the course of doing so, Ernest and Celestine draw the ire of both the bear and mice communities—Ernest has stolen, and Celestine has brought a bear into the mice's underground city.

They go on the run together, and the cover of snow keeps the police from finding them. When the snow melts, Ernest and Celestine are found by the police. When their good characters are proven in court, the judges agree to forgo the longstanding separation of mice and bears, and allow Ernest and Celestine to live together forever.

Together, Ernest and Celestine create a charming illustrated story of how they came to be a family, although they edit it to remove the fact that Ernest initially meant to eat Celestine.

The Adoption Connection

Ernest and Celestine form a cross-cultural family. They acknowledge to each other that they feel alone in the world, and Celestine shares that she does not have a home.

After their family is sanctioned in court, they go about creating the story of how they became a family. Their relationship could be viewed as either a parent–child relationship or a relationship between an older and younger sibling. Each acts reassuringly and with nurturance towards the other.

In the beginning of the film, Celestine is being raised in an orphanage.

Strong Points

It is heartwarming to see Ernest and Celestine grow from suspicion, to friends, to family. Some of their cultural upbringing still lingers, causing each to have a nightmare about the other's species, but Ernest and Celestine both remind each other that there is no truth to the nightmares.

Celestine is able to communicate her feelings through her drawings. In fact, it is her art that initially creates a sense of familial love between her and the artistically minded Ernest.

Challenges

The orphanage headmistress, The Gray One, tells the young mice a horrible bedtime story about the different ways bears like to eat mice. And, of course, Ernest does briefly try to eat Celestine.

Some young viewers might be scared to see Ernest and Celestine sitting in their cells, waiting for their trials while their captors appear to practice methods of execution.

Recommendations

Ernest and Celestine seems well-suited to viewers of ages 4–12.

The movie captures the development of a strong nurturing relationship between Ernest and Celestine, which eventually leads to the formation of a family. The fact that Ernest is a bear and Celestine is a mouse might be a useful touch point for families who have adopted cross-culturally, but the general size difference between Ernest and Celestine make the film likely to work for any adoption.

Many kids who have been adopted from foster care or from a group home will be able to see themselves in the role of Celestine—she is without a home and without a strong family connection. She is initially scared of the much larger Ernest, but finally feels at home with him.

Questions for Discussion

- When do you think Ernest and Celestine became a family?

- Ernest and Celestine look different from each other; what makes them a family?

- Did you ever feel scared like Celestine before you came to a new home? What helped you start to feel safe?

- Do you think Ernest is more like a dad or a big brother to Celestine?

- Was it OK for Ernest and Celestine to change some of their story? Why did they do it? What is the best way to handle the hard parts of the story about how a family was formed?

- For parents: What sort of things do your children draw? In what creative ways do they like to express themselves?

Family Activity

As a family activity, why not collaboratively write and illustrate an age-appropriate storybook about how your family was formed?

How to Train Your Dragon 2

(2014, PG, 102 minutes. Animated. Starring Jay
Baruchel, Cate Blanchet, and Gerard Butler)

The Plot

Five years ago, the Viking village of Berk made peace with nearby dragons; now, the Vikings and dragons co-exist joyfully. This was brought about by Hiccup, the nerdy son of village chief Stoick the Vast. Hiccup's skillful, loving partnerships with dragons were initially surprising and off-putting to Stoick, since the village valued warriors who battled dragons, but eventually Hiccup's approach won Stoick over.

Now Hiccup has turned 20 and Stoick is pressuring him to become the village's new chief. In the midst of this, the village's peace is threatened by Drago Bludvist, who intends to hypnotize and steal the dragons to build an army.

While working against Drago, Hiccup encounters another person who is skilled with dragons, and he comes to learn that it is Valka, his long-lost mother. Stoick arrives shortly afterwards, and the family is reunited for the first time since Hiccup's infancy. However, the reunion is tragically short-lived when Stoick is killed by a hypnotized dragon.

Now, with Valka's encouragement, Hiccup allows himself to be the village chief and works to defeat Drago and restore peace to the village.

The Adoption Connection

Hiccup never really knew his mother; at some point in his early childhood, she went away. Now, he meets her and finds that he has much in common with her. Hiccup gets to see his parents briefly reunited, but his father is killed shortly afterwards.

Hiccup struggles to understand his identity. He sees himself as being dissimilar to his father, and he has never met his mother. He is left wondering who he is. He eventually meets his mother and sees some of his characteristics reflected in her.

Hiccup initially does not realize that the woman he meets is his mother. Some people touched by adoption wonder whether they're ever in the presence of a blood relative without realizing it. When he acknowledges that it is difficult for him to grasp that she is his mother, she apologizes for being absent and asks for another chance to be his family.

Strong Points

Hiccup finds that some of his positive and unusual traits are actually shared with his mother. In meeting her he is able to better understand his identity and transition into adulthood.

Challenges

The concept of an unlikely parental reunion being cut short by a violent death might be very hard for some young viewers who have lost a parent.

Recommendations

Kids who have been adopted might wonder where some of their traits, characteristics, and talents come from. They might find it interesting to see that some of Hiccup's unique characteristics are shared with a parent who he has not known. Hiccup is able to progress into adulthood once he understands that he has a combination of traits from both of his parents.

This film might most appeal to kids of ages 8–14. It could be especially helpful for preteens and young teens who are in the process of figuring out their own identity or thinking about how unknown or absent birth parents influence who they are.

Questions for Discussion

- In what ways does Hiccup reflect Stoick? In what ways does he reflect Valka? In what ways is he unique from both of them? Does he reflect anyone else?

- What do you know about your birth parents? What do you imagine about them?

- What traits do you think you've gotten from your adoptive family? Which ones have you gotten from your birth family? Which ones have you gotten from your friends? Are there any you've developed on your own?

- How will Hiccup recover from the loss he experiences?

Kung Fu Panda

(2008, PG, 92 minutes. Animated. Starring Jack Black, Dustin Hoffman, Angelina Jolie, and Jackie Chan)

The Plot

Po the panda lives at the foot of the mountain where he helps his father, a goose named Mr. Ping, with his family noodle shop.

Po is a devoted fan of Kung Fu and particularly idolizes the Furious Five, a quintet of masters who live and train at the top of the mountain. When a tournament is announced to determine which of the Five will earn the Dragon Scroll, Po is desperate to attend—and is surprised when he is identified as the one worthy of the Dragon Scroll. Unfortunately, this also means that he's the one who will be expected to defeat Tai Lung, a dangerous villain whose vengeance-fueled return to the land is anticipated. And Po doesn't even know Kung Fu.

The Adoption Connection

Po has been adopted by Mr. Ping. We learn more of their story in *Kung Fu Panda 2*, but we already see that Po is loved by Mr. Ping. This film acknowledges that there is some tension in the family, but Po and Mr. Ping have never yet talked about the adoption. Mr. Ping is anxious for Po to become a noodle merchant, and tells him, "We're noodle folk. Broth runs through our veins." However, he does not become disappointed in Po when Po confesses that he's not as interested in noodles as he had pretended.

The Furious Five are trained by Master Shifu, who functions as an adoptive parent to them. Shifu did adopt Tai Lung, but now finds himself at odds with him. It's a rare movie in which both the hero and the villain are adopted.

Tigress, one of the Five, feels sad because Shifu did not show love to her—he was hurt by Tai Lung and seemed unwilling to love again. I think there could be a parallel here for foster parents who've experienced disrupted placements of children that they had hoped to adopt.

Strong Points

Shifu originally disparages Po but is inspired to try again and, with the conviction that he can successfully train Po, finds a way to motivate him. With the right motivation to learn, Po thrives and uses his unique gifts, which had originally appeared to be obstacles.

Even when he feels dejected, Po can go home to Mr. Ping, and Mr. Ping never stops believing in him.

Challenges

Po does not know about his adoption; it is alluded to but mostly for humor.

Recommendations

This film highlights the love of an adoptive father for his son, the sense that you can always come home, and the sense that you're special even when you feel as though you're not.

It's good for kids to have models of healthy, supportive adoptive families—and for some kids it might be especially important to have models of supportive, nurturing adoptive fathers. This fits nicely.

It seems good for kids of ages 5 and up.

Questions for Discussion

- What makes Mr. Ping a good dad?

- Why do you think Po doesn't know that he was adopted?

- Who was your favorite one of the Furious Five?

Kung Fu Panda 2

(2011, PG, 90 minutes. Animated. Starring Jack Black,
Dustin Hoffman, Angelina Jolie, and Jackie Chan)

The Plot

Years ago, the evil peacock, Lord Shen, heard a prophecy that threatened his defeat at the hands of a warrior of black and white if he did not change his evil ways. Instead of changing, Shen attempted to execute all pandas. At least one panda has survived. Po, the Kung Fu Panda, has been raised since infancy by his adoptive father, a goose named Mr. Ping.

Lord Shen has returned to exact revenge for his exile, and Po must try to fulfill the prophecy and defeat the villain. He also must learn how he came to be the son of Mr. Ping and discover the truth of his own identity.

The Adoption Connection

Po is the adopted son of Mr. Ping, and in this movie, we learn his story. Po's panda mother placed him in a basket of produce to keep him safe from an invading army. That basket was delivered to Mr. Ping's noodle shop; there, Mr. Ping discovered Po and raised him as his own son.

Po is triggered by a symbol that was present during a raid on his birth family's village, and it brings back unexpected and unwanted memories for him. This might be one of the clearest cinematic depictions of an emotional trigger, and this in itself might give parents a way to discuss triggers with their kids. Po has a nightmare that his birth parents have replaced him and do not care for him.

Po spends the whole movie trying to answer the question of who he actually is. Mr. Ping reminds him that his story has had a happy ending, but Po still needs to search to find the answers to his questions. His quest for knowledge about himself is palpably important to him.

Strong Points

Mr. Ping works through his discomfort with the conversation and gives Po the fullest explanation he can of Po's adoption story. Po takes some considerable time to integrate this information into his life and continues to remember and learn more details about his story. He ultimately embraces both parts of his identity; he is both the beloved son of a goose and the long-foretold of black and white warrior.

Challenges

Part of the story does involve the apparent genocide of pandas, including Po's birth family. Although some of them have survived, they have been exiled. There are some frightening scenes and implications that could be triggers for some kids.

When Mr. Ping tells Po about his adoption of Po, he acknowledges that although he waited for people to come to claim Po, no one did. Lord Shen even tries to manipulate Po by saying his parents abandoned him. Lord Shen also tells Po that Po's parents didn't love him. Some children might find this to be a story of abandonment, which could be difficult if they've felt that they were abandoned. Lord Shen's statement that he scarred Po for life by taking away his parents might also be a trigger to kids with unresolved or unexplored issues of loss.

Although it is an honest question of identity—and although it is resolved positively—there is a scene in which Mr. Ping and Po seem uncertain of whether Po is truly

Mr. Ping's son. It is left in question for the bulk of the movie. Po confides in a friend that he has learned that his dad isn't his real dad. By the end of the film, Po affirms that he is the son of Mr. Ping. I could imagine this question of identity and belonging being a hard theme for some kids. I could also imagine some parents treating this theme as unmentionable. However, questions of identity and belonging are real for many people touched by adoption, and a parent gently bringing it up as a topic of conversation might be helpful to a child.

Po has dreams that his birth parents have replaced him.

At one point, Po says that the past doesn't matter, but it seems that he will be proven wrong in a sequel; by the end of the film, we learn that Po's panda father is alive and has learned that Po lives.

Recommendations

This one seems best suited to kids of ages 9–12 and some teens.

It might be triggering for kids with unresolved or unexplored issues of loss or abandonment, but it could also be helpful for exploring questions of identity. By the end of the film, Po has learned much (but not all!) of his story and has developed a more integrated identity.

This film could also be helpful for parents who want to understand or explain triggers.

Questions for Discussion

- Po saw something that brought back a lot of painful memories and feelings to him. Has anything like that ever happened to you?

- Why did Po's panda parents send him away?

- How many parents does Po have?

- Have you ever wondered who you are?

- Can you be the child of both your adoptive parents and birth parents?

- If you could ask your birth parents anything, what would it be?

- Is it possible that more than one set of parents love you at the same time?

Kung Fu Panda 3

(2016, PG, 95 minutes. Animated. Starring Jack Black, Dustin Hoffman, Angelina Jolie, J. K. Simmons, and Jackie Chan)

The Plot

Po the panda has been named as the teacher for the Furious Five, a team of martial artists whom he once idolized (and of whom he still has action figures). He struggles to teach them and begins doubting himself. His former teacher, Master Shifu, advises him that Po needs to be himself, rather than trying to be someone else—but Po believes that he does not know who he is.

Po has not seen his birth father since Po was very young, but his birth father (Li Shen) arrives at the noodle shop owned by Po's adoptive father, Mr. Ping. Mr. Ping is initially jealous, and Li Shen seems to discount Mr. Ping, but together, Li Shen, Po, and Mr. Ping travel to a secret panda village. There, Li Shen promises that Po will learn what it means to be a panda and also how to harness the power of

Chi, which Po needs to learn in order to defeat his latest foe. While Po is learning about his panda heritage, he must also prepare to face a spirit warrior named Kai who has returned from beyond the grave to assert his dominance over all other Kung Fu masters.

The Adoption Connection

Kung Fu Panda 3 continues Po's discovery of his adoption story. His birth father, Li Shen, unexpectedly arrives in his life. Po is awestruck and overjoyed at meeting his birth father, but his adoptive father is initially suspicious and jealous.

Later, Li Shen confides to Mr. Ping that he is scared of losing Po again, and Mr. Ping confides the same feeling to Li Shen. Together, they realize that they both love Po, and that neither one replaces the other.

Eventually, both dads defend Po from his enemies, using what they dub a "Double Dad Defense." While Po's two fathers learn what it will mean to share Po, Po learns his birth name and what it means to be a panda.

Eventually, Po answers the question of identity that he has wrestled with for so long. Is he the son of a panda or the son of a goose? Is he a student, a teacher, or a friend? His final answer: he is all of these things.

Po initially struggles to know what to call Li Shen.

Strong Points

Taken together, the *Kung Fu Panda* trilogy has a wonderfully healthy and positive adoption storyline. Po initially does not know he is adopted. Mr. Ping tells Po about how he found, raised, and adopted him. Po then meets his birth father and learns about his personal history and panda culture. He is amazed to meet a community of individuals who look like him. Then, he integrates all aspects of his identity into a cohesive whole, while he watches his two dads successfully navigate their new relationship with each other.

Not only does Po learn about panda culture, but he also shares his Kung Fu culture and his noodle shop culture with the pandas. Together the community comes together, celebrating and learning from each other with each member also drawing strength from their individual uniqueness. There's a lot of mutual respect and assistance: Po saves everyone and then they all save him.

The film does not shy away from the awkwardness and mistrust that Mr. Ping and Li Shen initially feel towards each other, but shows them working through that uncomfortable start to a place of trusting and humble relationship. Mr. Ping ultimately acknowledges that he thought that having Li Shen in Po's life would mean less of Po's love for Mr. Ping, but now, Mr. Ping realizes that it means more love for Po.

Challenges

While Po is uncertain of what to call Li Shen, Mr. Ping initially seems to try to steer Po away from calling him "Dad."

Both dads have kept truth from Po. In an attempt to protect Po, Li Shen lies to him. Mr. Ping (who is a goose) acknowledges that Po still thinks he was hatched from an egg. Mr. Ping jokes that he has proven his ability to keep secrets, since Po was 20 years old before he learned of his adoption.

Po never gets to meet his birth mother; she died before he found the pandas. He does get to learn about her, as Li Shen talks about her in glowing terms.

In a moment of anger, Po implies to Li Shen that their relationship is over, but his anger does not last. Mr. Ping tenderly tells Li Shen that Po will not be out of Li Shen's life forever.

Mr. Ping acknowledges that parents lie to their children at times, but that it is a case of doing something wrong while having genuinely good intentions. Sometimes, adoptive parents hide a child's adoption from them. As in this story, it's a case of good intentions leading to a potentially hurtful decision.

Recommendations

Kung Fu Panda 3 finishes one of the healthiest cinematic portrayals of a newly opened adoption. The film is entertaining and positive and will please most kids, teens, and adults.

It provides rich material for several conversations and seems well suited to all viewers of ages 5 and up. Younger children might be scared by some fight scenes, but might also enjoy the film.

Questions for Discussion

- What do you think Po should call Li Shen? What should he call Mr. Ping? Does it matter whether he uses the same name for both of them? How should he decide what to do?

- What do you think it would be like to meet your birth family? How would you like your adoptive family and your birth family to treat each other?

- Po is a warrior, a teacher, a student, the son of Li Shen, and the son of Mr. Ping. What different roles make you who you are?

- Is it more important to find out what your roots are or to function as the person you are today, or are they both important? How does finding out your roots help you be who you are?

- What happened when Mr. Ping found Po and took him in? Did Po start being Mr. Ping's son? Did he ever stop being Li Shen's son?

- Should Mr. Ping or Li Shen have lied to Po? What happened because they did? What would have been a better choice for them to make?

Mr. Peabody and Sherman

(2014, PG, 92 minutes. Animated. Starring Ty Burrell, Max Charles, and Ariel Winter)

The Plot

The highly accomplished dog, Mr. Peabody, is the adoptive father of seven-year-old human Sherman. During an argument at school, a bully named Penny calls Sherman a dog and taunts him. Sherman bites her. This draws the attention of Child Protective Services worker Ms. Grunion, who asserts that a dog cannot raise a human child. Even though Peabody fought hard to earn the legal right to adopt Sherman, Ms. Grunion vows to remove Sherman from his home.

Before Ms. Grunion makes her visit, Peabody invites Penny's parents over in an attempt to make peace with them. While the adults are talking, Sherman and Penny go on adventures in Peabody's time machine. They become friends, but Ms. Grunion is still bent on taking Sherman away from

Peabody. When she tries to take Sherman from the home physically, Peabody bites her. She seems happy about this, because it seems likely to prove her point that Peabody is an unfit parent. She calls the police and animal control to come and get Peabody.

The time machine causes chaos that delays Peabody's capture, and Sherman asserts that Peabody is a loyal and good father. Although Ms. Grunion is still set against Peabody, she is kidnapped by an ancient soldier who takes her away from Peabody for good. Peabody is pardoned, and he and Sherman are able to continue in their life as father and son, with Sherman now proud to be the son of a dog.

The Adoption Connection

Peabody grew up in an adoption center, but was never chosen because he was bookish rather than doggish. He became very successful in business, science, and art. One day, he saw the infant Sherman, abandoned in a box. Peabody recognized himself in Sherman, took him in, and began to raise him. Although there was no legal precedent for Peabody to adopt Sherman, Peabody fought for—and won—the right to do that.

Sherman struggles with his feelings regarding being part of a canine family, but eventually accepts it when he realizes that Peabody is such a loyal and loving person.

Some lighthearted jokes are made about the fact that Peabody and Sherman do not look like each other. Characters explain it by saying that it's an adoptive family.

Strong Points

Peabody cares deeply for Sherman. He has fought for his right to adopt Sherman and fights to keep him; at the same time, he assures Sherman that he will not let him be taken away, and tells him that it is not Sherman's job to worry. It is helpful for kids to know that their parents will take care of the things that concern the children.

Challenges

Sherman faces many potential losses. Some children might find the concept of a social worker trying to divide an adoptive family to be too emotionally difficult to enjoy. It could be very difficult for some kids to watch a movie in which the permanency of an adoption is not something that can be depended upon.

Kids who remember being removed from a home might be triggered by these scenes to remember traumatic events from their own childhoods.

There are two scenes in which it appears briefly that Peabody has died.

Although Peabody loves Sherman deeply, he struggles to tell him so, prefers not to be called "Dad," and on one occasion says that Sherman is very bad. By the end of the film, he is able to tell Sherman that he loves him.

Recommendations

For some children, this isn't a good choice because of the threat to Peabody's adoption of Sherman. The other elements described above might also make the film difficult to watch for some.

For kids who won't be bothered by the concerns listed above, the film does offer the opportunity to explore Sherman's feelings about being different from his dad and to portray the dedication that a parent and child can have for each other.

Because of the concerns, the film probably isn't a good fit for younger viewers and might be best suited to kids of ages 11–13.

Parents would want to assure their kids that their adoption is permanent and could reaffirm that, as Peabody does for Sherman, they would do anything to keep their family together and to protect their child.

Questions for Discussion

- Why was Penny being so mean to Sherman? How do you think Sherman felt?

- Have you ever been bullied? Has it ever been about adoption, or about our family, or about appearances? Can you decide whether to take what a bully says as truth?

- Was Sherman embarrassed to be Peabody's son, or was he just reacting to the unkind way Penny was treating him?

- Do you think most social workers are like Ms. Grunion? Have you ever known any adults who were mean like her? What were your social workers like?

- How can Sherman be Peabody's son without being a dog? Is he a dog?

- If you had a time machine, what times would you like to visit?

Paddington

(2014, PG, 95 minutes. Live Action. Starring Hugh Bonneville, Sally Hawkins, Peter Capaldi, and Nicole Kidman)

The Plot

Years ago, an English explorer discovered a new species of bear in Peru. When the explorer realized that the bears could learn English, he named them Pastuzo and Lucy and told them they would be welcome if they ever wanted to come to London.

Pastuzo and Lucy have been living with their young nephew Paddington. When a storm destroys their home and takes away Pastuzo, Lucy tells Paddington that he should go to London to find a home. Paddington goes with a tag around his neck, hoping that a family will adopt him.

He is taken in by the Brown family who promise to help him find a home, although Mr. Brown is uncomfortable about having a bear in the home. Paddington believes that he would be able to live with the explorer who initially discovered his relatives, and Mr. Brown helps Paddington learn the name of that explorer.

When Paddington's adventures leave the Browns' home in a mess, Paddington overhears the Browns talking and believes that he is no longer welcome in their home. He sets out on his own to discover the explorer, but instead finds the explorer's daughter, who is a cruel scientist set on killing and stuffing Paddington. The Browns learn of Paddington's danger and set off to save him; in doing so, they realize that they would like to be his family.

The Adoption Connection

Paddington is sent to London in search of a new family after a disaster destroys his home, leaving his elderly aunt unable to care for him.

Paddington is taken in by the Browns, who initially intend to care for him only temporarily. Paddington searches for information about his family's past that he believes will help him find a home but eventually becomes a part of the Brown family. Mrs. Brown gives Paddington an English name (his original name is a series of growls that the Browns cannot pronounce correctly) and he becomes a part of their family.

In a way, the Browns serve as a foster family for Paddington while he is trying to reunify with the explorer who knew his relatives. When the reunification fails, Paddington is able to stay with the Browns, since they have already developed a bond with each other.

Strong Points

The film acknowledges that people need more than just a roof and a bed to feel at home.

One character explains that it can be difficult to be new in an environment.

By the end of the film, it is evident that even though Paddington brings some chaos to the Brown home, they are better off having him in their lives. This could be helpful reassurance for kids and parents who felt as though their introduction to their new family was less than ideal. It can still work out!

Mr. Brown eventually declares that, even though there are differences between Paddington and the rest of his family,

Paddington is part of their family and family bonds are unbreakable. Paddington expresses that he is not bothered by the differences between himself and the Browns because he has found a home with them.

Challenges

The Browns briefly talk about an orphanage. As they talk, an image of a frightening house flashes onscreen for a moment.

Paddington runs away from the Brown home after overhearing Mr. and Mrs. Brown saying that they think Paddington does not fit with their family because they believe he is lying to them about the day's events. Mr. Brown frequently misjudges Paddington as being unsafe and dishonest.

Some viewers might find it hard to watch a scene in which Paddington is alone in a subway trying to find a family, as well as some scenes in which Mr. Brown expresses his doubts about having Paddington in the home.

Kids who find themselves identifying with Paddington might be saddened when his aunt sends him away and scared when a cruel scientist expresses her intention to kill Paddington.

Recommendations

Paddington seems most likely to be helpful to kids of ages 8–12; younger kids might be scared by the villainous intentions of the cruel scientist.

The film might particularly be helpful for kids adopted from foster care by their foster family, since Paddington also became a permanent part of a family in whose home his presence was initially expected to be temporary.

After watching this, consider talking about how your family grew to include your kids. It may also be helpful to comment that neither Paddington nor the Browns initially expected themselves to grow into a family. The Browns thought Paddington was a temporary guest, Paddington initially had no expectations of who would become his family, and later he thought he would live with the explorer. Even though this family was not their initial intention, they all gladly accept it. It can be that way in foster care adoptions, as well!

Questions for Discussion

- Has a grown-up ever thought you were lying when you were really telling the truth? How does it feel when someone does believe you, even if the true story you are telling is hard to believe?

- Are there any parts of your birth family's past (or your adoptive family's past) that feel mysterious to you? What questions do you have?

- In what ways is adoption what you expected? In what ways is it different?

- What makes where you live feel like a home?

Penguins of Madagascar

(2014, PG, 92 minutes. Animated. Starring Tom McGrath, Christopher Knights, and Benedict Cumberbatch)

The Plot

Ten years ago, the penguins Skipper, Rico, and Kowalski rescued an egg that hatched into a baby penguin they named Private. Now, they view the clumsy Private as a mascot, but Private wants to be viewed as a respected and valued member of their team and family.

When a villain tries to take revenge on all penguins, Private rises to the occasion and acts with bravery and selflessness. He is scarred, but earns the respect he has longed for.

The Adoption Connection

Skipper, Rico, and Kowalski combine to form a nurturing family for Private. While one of them tells Private that, technically, he has no family, another suggests that because they have each other, they are a family. One character refers to the others as his brothers.

Strong Points

Private exceeds others' expectations of him. He is hurt by their low expectations of him, but he does not let those expectations define him. Even when his brothers don't respect him, they still love him. By the end of the film, he has both their love and their respect.

Challenges

Scenes in which Private is separated from his family could be scary to some young viewers.

Recommendations

Sometimes, members of a family find themselves playing a certain role in the family; perhaps someone is the calming one, the delicate one, the funny one, or the troubled one (psychologists might refer to someone in the family being the "identified patient"). The role assignments might be based in reality and might happen unintentionally, but they are still felt throughout the family.

This film shows how one character feels undervalued by the role he has been placed in. Watching this film could open up a discussion about family roles.

Kids and preteens might be most likely to enjoy it, but teenagers might also be interested in talking about family roles, especially as they consider new ones. This one could work for ages 3–17.

Questions for Discussion

- Private's role in his family was to be cute. What do you think his role will be now?

- What role do you feel that you have in our family? How do you feel about the role?

- What's the difference between being loved and being respected? What does it feel like to have both in the same relationship?

Rio 2

(2014, G, 101 minutes. Animated. Starring Anne
Hathaway, Jesse Eisenberg, and Kristin Chenoweth)

The Plot

Blu and Jewel believe that they and their children are the
only blue macaws in existence. They have been cared for in
Rio de Janeiro by married scientists Tulio and Linda and
appear to be quite comfortable. Blu and his kids enjoy their
life. Jewel, who remembers life in the jungle, is dismayed
to realize that her family is living more like humans than
like macaws.

When Jewel learns that Linda and Tulio have discovered
other blue macaws in the jungle, she desires to find them.
Blu, Jewel, their children, and some friends travel from
Rio de Janeiro to the jungle and are amazed to realize
that the macaws they've been looking for are Jewel's long-
lost family. Her father, Eduardo, is the chief of the birds
and gladly welcomes Jewel back. He is delighted to meet
his grandchildren, but is unimpressed with Blu and treats
him coldly.

Blu struggles to fit in with the macaws while Jewel and
the children thrive there. In the meantime, an old nemesis of
Blu has come to the jungle to exact revenge. Another danger
is that the macaw habitat is under threat from a group of
illegal loggers who have kidnapped Tulio and Linda to
prevent them from stopping the logging operation.

When Jewel's father realizes Blu's bravery and the
trustworthiness of Blu's human friends, he warms to Blu. Blu
and Jewel ultimately decide to live in the jungle with Jewel's
family, but also intend to spend their summers back in Rio.

The Adoption Connection

Blu has spent years living under human care, and he has become acculturated to human life. Jewel loves Blu but doesn't want being in a relationship with him to cause her to lose ties to her more traditional macaw lifestyle. The blending of multiple cultures into one family has potential relevance for many adoptive families, whether it's the blending of cultures from two nations or the blending of cultures from two different families from the same region.

Jewel had thought that she would never see her childhood family again and was thrilled to find them. Her father was overjoyed to meet his grandchildren. Some adult adoptees started thinking about their adoption more in earnest when they themselves became parents, and might find that they resonate with Jewel.

Some adoptive parents might be scared that they would not fit in with people from their child's birth family or birth culture, and they might resonate with Blu's nervousness and anxiety around Jewel's father.

Kids adopted cross-culturally or kids of adopted parents might find the film interesting for its depiction of the reunification between Jewel and her family, as well as its depiction of a family working to blend two different cultures.

Strong Points

This film shows that a family can successfully incorporate a new culture, although it takes love and understanding.

Although Jewel wants to remain with her family, she firmly asserts that Blu is also her family and she refuses to leave him.

Challenges

Blu and his family have a strong sense of loyalty to each other, but he struggles to develop or understand a similar sense of loyalty to Jewel's family. His strong but narrow definition of family makes him want to ask Jewel to limit her ties with her family. Fortunately, by the end of the film, Blu has begun to see himself as part of the macaw family.

It's interesting to notice that in order to make room for Jewel's relationships with her childhood family, Blu had to come to see himself as part of that family as well. Perhaps a similar dynamic is true in adoptive families; to embrace openness, adoptive parents might need to be able to conceptualize themselves as part of their child's extended birth family.

It might be hard for some kids to hear Jewel's father tearfully recount how Jewel was separated from the rest of her family.

Jewel's family initially has a hard time accepting Blu. Her father disagrees with Blu about Blu's relationship with Tulio and Linda, saying that humans cannot be family.

An attractive friend of Jewel's suggests that he would marry Jewel if Blu ever died.

Recommendations

Rio 2 seems likely to appeal to a couple of different audiences. Kids of ages 4–9 might enjoy it as a fun film. Preteens, teenagers, and adults could benefit from its portrayal of reunification and merging cultures.

Questions for Discussion (for Kids)

- What do you think it felt like for Blu and Jewel to realize that they weren't all alone, after all?

- Do you think Blu is part of Jewel's family now? If so, when did that happen? If not, what needs to happen to make it so?

- How many cultures are represented in our family? Are there any cultures you would like us to add or explore?

Questions for Discussion (for Parents)

- How do you view the connection between you and your child's extended birth family? Are they on your family tree? Do you think of them as family, friends, strangers, or adversaries?

- How would each different conceptualization of your child's extended birth family impact your relationship with them?

- How would your kids' experience change if you conceptualized their birth family differently?

- How can you and those who care about the children in your home help your child or your child's birth family as they try to integrate two different cultures?

- What parts of cultural integration are scary or threatening?

- Blu felt the need to prove himself to Jewel and seemed to fear losing her. Are you scared that you might lose your child's love if you are involved with your child's birth family or birth culture? It is a common and understandable fear, but is it likely to be realistic?

Teenage Mutant Ninja Turtles

(2014, PG-13, 101 minutes. Live Action.
Starring Megan Fox and Will Arnett)

The Plot

The evil Foot Clan gang is terrorizing New York City. A sinister businessman named Sacks is secretly working to help them develop a biological weapon and hopes to become rich by selling the cure once the weapon is unleashed.

Local news reporter April O'Neal is investigating the Foot Clan and is shocked to see them bested by an unknown vigilante. When her investigations bring her dangerously close to the action, April is held hostage by the Foot Clan, but is rescued by the vigilante and three others like him. April learns that the vigilantes are four human-sized turtles who have been trained in ninjutsu.

In time, April realizes that the four turtles, Leonardo, Donatello, Raphael, and Michelangelo, are four of her childhood pets; they had been kept in Sacks' lab, where April's father worked. When the lab burned down, April freed her pets and a lab rat named Splinter into the sewers. Substances from the lab caused the animals to become human-like; Splinter grew first and so assumed a parental role for the turtles. When April meets Splinter, he explains that the turtles have become his sons; he raised them and taught them how to be ninjas. Splinter also reveals to April that Sacks killed her father.

April and the turtles join together with the hopes of stopping Sacks' evil work and thwarting the Foot Clan, but the Foot Clan has tracked April to the turtles' hideout. The Foot Clan captures three of the turtles and injures Splinter. April and Raphael must work together to thwart the Foot Clan and must also save Splinter and rescue Raphael's brothers.

The Adoption Connection

Several characters experienced adoption by a father figure or the loss of a father. Splinter has become an adoptive father to the turtles and has taught them a strong sense of family loyalty; the calling card that the turtles use to represent themselves is a Japanese symbol meaning "family."

April's father died when she was young; we aren't told anything about her mother.

As a child, Sacks was taken in by a sensei who filled a paternal role for him; that sensei later became known as Shredder, the leader of the Foot Clan. It's because of this connection that Sacks is collaborating with the gang.

Strong Points

Splinter is an excellent father; he claims the turtles as his sons, teaches them how to protect themselves and others, and continually affirms them, telling them that they are exceptional and communicating his belief to them that they will do great things for the common good.

Though Splinter is strict at times, he reminds the turtles that they must trust him and believe in each other. They thrive under his parenting and honor him with love, respect, and devotion. Splinter responds to the turtles' teenage immaturity with both humor and firmness. Splinter also shares with April that he learned about being a father from watching how April's father loved her.

Challenges

April learns about her father's murder; this could be difficult for kids who have lost parents.

For a short time, it seems as though Shredder has killed Splinter.

Three of the turtles are confined in cages while a villain drains their blood; this could be difficult for kids who have been confined during the course of being abused.

April is told that her father will be proud of her as long as she does what she thinks is right; it's decent advice on the surface, but it comes from Sacks, who murdered her father.

One character mocks Splinter and the turtles, suggesting that they cannot really be a family.

Recommendations

This is a movie about both an adoptive father raising four sons and the powerful bond between siblings.

This film seems helpful for normalizing adoption; Splinter and the turtles are depicted as a strong family, and there is some talk of how they became a family, but adoption isn't the plot of the story. There is an emphasis on family loyalty. Splinter's high opinion and high expectations of his sons can be inspiring.

Teenage Mutant Ninja Turtles seems best suited to kids of ages 9–13.

Questions for Discussion

- What are some of the important ways that the turtles were influenced by Splinter? In what way was Sacks influenced by Shredder?

- If you were one of the turtles, what would your name be?

- What do you and your siblings have in common? Do you have any friends who are like siblings to you?

- What's the best part about having siblings? Or what do you imagine would be the best thing about having siblings?

Family Activity

Working together, create a design or a mark that can symbolize your family. When you're happy with it, frame it! If you design it on a computer, you could even use an online printing service to make it look extra nice!

Turbo

(2013, PG, 96 minutes. Animated. Starring Ryan Reynolds, Paul Giamatti, Snoop Dogg, and Samuel L. Jackson)

The Plot

A garden snail named Theo dreams of being a world-class racer like his hero, the Indy 500 champion racecar driver Guy Gagné.

After being mocked by other snails, a rejected Theo experiences a freak series of events that leave him with super speed. His super speed initially is a hazard, and it results in Theo and his brother Chet being fired from their jobs.

Shortly after being fired, Chet is captured by crows, but Theo uses his super speed to pursue them and rescues Chet in the parking lot of a mini mall. There they are captured by a human named Tito.

Tito is amazed by Theo's speed, and Theo convinces Tito to enter him into the Indy 500. Racing under the name Turbo, Theo is mocked by other competitors but manages to qualify for the race, in which he will go head-to-head with his former hero, Guy Gagné. To win, he'll need help from his friends and the support of his brother.

The Adoption Connection

A chaotic event results in Theo travelling with his brother to a new community. Together, they find a new group of friends, which becomes somewhat of a family to them, and Theo takes on a new name.

Strong Points

It takes Chet some time, but he eventually gives Theo the emotional support that Theo needs to achieve his dream.

Challenges

The racer that Theo has idolized doesn't live up to his expectations.

Recommendations

Although *Turbo* isn't an adoption story, there is an aspect in which some young viewers might see reflections of their own stories, as Turbo and his brother travel together to a new home and a new life.

Turbo is a fun, light movie that seems most likely to appeal to kids of ages 3–8.

Questions for Discussion

- How many different names and nicknames have you had?

- How special was it to Turbo that Chet always stayed with him?

- Who has been connected to you for your whole life?

- What do you think Turbo and Chet remember about their first home? What do you think they like best about their new home?

- If you could have any super power, what would you choose?

Chapter 7

MOVIES TO WATCH WITH YOUR TEENS

Teenagers are in the business of figuring out who they are and who they want to be; adoption can add more layers of complexity to that task. Here are several movies that seem likely to appeal to teenagers and preteens as well. The questions are largely geared towards some higher-level, deeper topics that could be helpful for teens to process with you, using these movies as launching platforms and reference points. The questions in this section center on thoughts regarding birth family members and reunification, processing loss, defining family, dealing with Confidentiality and Secrecy, developing a blended identity, understanding the circumstances of one's adoption, addressing feelings of guilt, family trees, and questions that teens wish they could ask of people with whom they have lost contact.

Closure

(2013, Not rated, 76 minutes. Documentary. Directed
by Bryan Tucker and starring Angela Tucker)
Award: 2014 Adoption at the Movies Award
for Best Smaller-Scale Release

The Plot

Angela was born in Tennessee. She was relinquished shortly
after her birth, and after a brief time in a foster home, she was
adopted by the Burt family in Washington State. Angela's
adoption was a "closed" adoption, so any information in the
birth records provided to her adoptive family that would
have identified her birth family was redacted. When the
Burts adopted Angela, doctors feared that she would never
walk; however, Angela thrived, and far exceeded the doctors'
expectations.

Angela has long held a curiosity about her birth family.
As a recently married twenty something, Angela decides to
try to discover her history and find her birth parents. Angela
is supported and accompanied by her adoptive family and
her filmmaker husband as they travel to Tennessee in hopes
of meeting Angela's birth parents.

Although Angela's birth mother initially denies Angela,
Angela is immediately embraced by her birth father, his
entire extended family, and the extended family of her birth
mother. Eventually, Angela's birth mother also embraces her
and explains the reason for her initial reaction.

As the documentary comes to a close, Angela has entered
into meaningful relationships with many of her birth family
members and has the full support of her adoptive family
and husband. The closure she sought opens the possibility of
many positive, ongoing relationships.

The Adoption Connection

Angela was adopted as a baby. She loves her adoptive family and also wants to find her birth family. At least one member of her adoptive family is initially uncomfortable with Angela's desire to find her birth family, but eventually they all support her and Angela acknowledges that she could not imagine going on this journey of discovery without them.

Although she was only hoping to find her birth parents, Angela also found many other relatives. She also learns that her mother relinquished one other child—and now, Angela, her birth sister, and her birth mother express their hope to find that family member as well.

Strong Points

Angela's adoptive family make her quest their own. As Angela and her husband buy tickets for their first trip to Tennessee, we see the box that indicates the number of tickets ordered; the cursor hovers over one before scrolling to six. Angela is not alone and expresses how touched she is that her family chose to accompany her on her journey.

Angela's adoptive mother expressed that she was motivated by a desire to be supportive of Angela. She has a deep conviction that Angela's search will not change her status as Angela's mom, and this allows her to join in Angela's desire for knowledge.

Angela's birth mother expresses that her family now includes Angela's adoptive family.

Angela's birth father is very happy to learn that he has a daughter, and his family welcome her as one of their own even before a DNA test confirms their relation.

Although Angela's birth mother initially rejects her, she later apologizes and acknowledges that she knew who Angela was as soon as she saw her.

Closure focuses on Angela and also has a wider perspective that shows the impact of her search on her birth and adoptive siblings, her extended families, and even her former foster family.

It's powerful to see Angela's two mothers embrace and thank each other.

Every year, Angela's adoptive family sent pictures and letters to the office in Tennessee that handled Angela's adoption. They had hoped Angela's birth mother would receive them. She had never received them, and so Angela and her adoptive family are able to go with her as she finally gets the packages and sees many years' worth of pictures for the first time.

Challenges

Angela's birth mother reports that she was never able to hold Angela because professionals told her that holding onto Angela would be "devastating" to her. I wonder if a different approach by the professionals working with Angela's birth mother could have reduced the suffering she felt after relinquishing Angela.

Recommendations

Closure is an excellent example of an adopted person seeking to reconnect with their birth family while also remaining fully a part of their adoptive family. The film honestly shares Angela's expectations, hopes, and worries, and also shares the honest feelings of those who love her.

This film seems most likely to appeal to viewers of ages 12 and up and is also a very good choice for adoptive parents and people considering becoming adoptive parents. As you watch it, consider the importance of your child's birth parents, and consider how you would be supportive if your child expressed the same needs that Angela felt.

Questions for Discussion

- Why do you think Angela wanted to find her birth mother?

- What fears might Angela's adoptive family have had about her finding her birth family? Were those fears realized?

- How might Angela's experience have been different had her adoptive family not been supportive of her desire to find her birth family?

- One of Angela's adoptive sisters acknowledged that she initially thought that Angela's desire to find her birth family was insulting to her adoptive parents, since she felt that it implied that Angela's adoptive parents were not sufficient. Angela affirms that she considers her adoptive parents to be her parents, but that she also wants to know her birth family. Does Angela's desire to find her birth family mean that her adoptive parents have not been sufficient family for her?

- Why did Deborah initially deny that Angela was her daughter? Was it worth Angela's continued efforts to connect with her?

Creed

(2015, PG-13, 133 minutes. Live Action. Starring
Michael B. Jordan and Sylvester Stallone)
Awards: 2016 Adoption at the Movies Awards Best Foster
or Adoptive Family and Best Foster or Adoptive Parent

The Plot

It's 1998 and Donnie Johnson is a youngster in trouble. He is serving time at a youth detention center and is in isolation for getting into fights. Mary Anne Creed finds Donnie at the center and offers to let him live with her.

Donnie has never known who his father was, but Mary Anne reveals to him that his father is also Mary Anne's late husband, boxing champion Apollo Creed.

Donnie lives with Mary Anne throughout his childhood and into his adulthood but eventually decides to set off on his own and become a professional boxer to follow in the footsteps of the famous father he never knew.

The Adoption Connection

Donnie is the son who resulted from an extramarital affair of Apollo Creed and a woman who we do not know. Mary Anne takes Donnie into her home and becomes a mother to him.

Donnie must figure out what it means to be the son of his father, even though he has never met him. Mary Anne, who does not want to see Donnie get injured in a boxing match, reminds him that although he is Apollo's son, he does not have to follow in all of Apollo's footsteps.

Donnie intentionally avoids using his father's last name at first because he wants to create his own legacy, but he eventually starts using his father's last name.

Donnie reconnects with his father's old friend, Rocky Balboa, and comes to call him an uncle.

One character suggests that Donnie is angry at his father for dying. Donnie later is asked what he would say to his father if he could; he says that he loves his father and understands that he did not intend to leave Donnie alone.

Strong Points

Donnie finds a patient, understanding, persevering, and supportive family in both Mary Anne and in Rocky. He embraces his family heritage while also crafting his own identity.

Challenges

Some people refer to Donnie as a mistake or an embarrassment, since he was born out of an affair. Mary Anne does not share these views but Donnie acknowledges that he feels pressure to prove that he is not a mistake.

Rocky hurts Donnie's feelings by saying that they are not really a family. He later redresses this and his familial relationship with Donnie seems likely to continue.

Mary Anne seems to kick Donnie out, telling him that if he wants to box, he shouldn't call her.

Recommendations

Creed seems likely to appeal to adults and some teenagers. It's an engaging story about a boxer developing his career, but the heart of the story is Donnie's work to embrace his father's history while also embracing his own individuality.

This one is best suited for teens ages 15 and up and their parents.

Questions for Discussion

- How much of a person's future is dictated by their family's history? How much of your life has been influenced by people you have never met?

- How far back can you trace your birth and adoptive family trees? Which people who aren't part of either of your family trees are still "like family" to you?

- What defines a "real family"? Is there value to the term, or would another term or set of terms be better?

- If you could say anything to a family member with whom you've lost contact, or whom you've never met, who would it be, and what would you say?

Divergent

(2014, PG-13, 139 minutes. Live Action. Starring
Shailene Woodley, Theo James, and Kate Winslet)

The Plot

In a dystopian future, the population of Chicago has been split into five communities. Each community is defined by a predominant character trait. Some people—the Factionless—are not defined by any character trait, and so live on the outskirts of society. Other people, Divergents, have multiple defining traits, but they have been forced into hiding by a government that fears that they cannot be controlled or trusted.

Beatrice Prior is a young Divergent, but her traits have remained hidden. Beatrice lives with her family in the Abnegation community; the Abnegation community has responsibility for governing Chicago and is also self-denying.

Now that Beatrice is 16 years old, she must choose, along with all the other 16-year-olds, whether to remain in her own community or join one of the other four. She is free to choose, but she is cautioned that her choice is irrevocable, and the community she chooses will have priority even over her family. Beatrice chooses to leave the community of her childhood to join the fearless community, Dauntless.

While there, Beatrice changes her name to Tris. She violates rules to visit her family members and learns that her childhood community and her parents are in danger, as another community intends to overthrow Abnegation from governing power.

Tris sees that the other Dauntless members are being brainwashed to kill members of Abnegation, but because Tris is Divergent, she is not susceptible to the brainwashing.

Tris falls into danger. Her mother is killed in the process of rescuing Tris. Later, Tris' father dies in an effort to stop the overthrow. With both of her parents killed, Tris joins with Four, a young man who has been training her, and together they stop the uprising.

The Adoption Connection

When Beatrice chooses to become a Dauntless, she must leave her community and family of origin and takes on a new name. While the choice is fully her own, it is supposed to be lifelong and irrevocable.

There is a strong theme of identity woven into the community at large; people are organized by their personality traits, and the most important thing people can do is to find where they fit. Any teen might ask themselves whether they fit in with their family, and adopted teens might deal with that question on multiple levels.

Adopted teens also must choose whether to leave their past completely behind or to find a way to work towards integrating all aspects of their identities. Tris would have been stifled by an artificially abbreviated identity.

Strong Points

Although her society wants her to choose one singular identity (one family, one community, one personality trait), Tris strives for an integrated identity, holding onto her past and her future.

Challenges

To choose their new community, teenagers slice their hand open and let their blood drip onto a symbol of their chosen community; it could be problematic for some teenagers to see self-harming behaviors portrayed as an honored ritual.

Some brutal teen-on-teen violence is hard to watch.

Tris' parents are both killed, which might stir some feelings of sadness for viewers who have lost parents or who worry about parents that they have lost contact with. Tris' mother dies in her arms.

Recommendations

Divergent can serve as a bridge into conversations with teens about their developing identities. Parents can draw parallels between Tris' transfer from one faction to another and an adopted person's transition from one family and culture to another.

Conversations about your teen's developing identity can also look at how your teen has incorporated adoption into their identity. This film can lead to talks about developing an integrated identity that incorporates a person's membership in both their birth family and their adoptive family.

This one seems best for kids of ages 12–16.

Questions for Discussion

- In what ways are you divergent, with regard to your personality?

- When someone is adopted, do they become divergent with regard to family membership, or do they have to choose only one "faction" to belong to?

- Tris has to face her biggest fears. What are some fears that you've confronted? How did you do it?

- In what ways can fear be helpful?

Man of Steel

(2013, PG-13, 143 minutes. Live Action. Starring Henry Cavill, Amy Adams, Kevin Costner, Laurence Fishburne, and Russell Crowe)
Award: 2014 Adoption at the Movies Awards, Film of the Year

The Plot

When their planet is in danger of destruction, Jor-El and Lara place their infant son Kal-El in a vessel programmed to take him safely to another world. Shortly after Kal-El is sent away, the planet Krypton explodes. The only surviving Kryptonians are Kal-El and a group of prisoners led by General Zod who are intent on capturing him.

Kal-El lands safely on Earth, where he is found by a childless couple, Jonathan and Martha Kent. The Kents adopt him and name him Clark.

Clark has superhuman abilities that the Kents encourage him to keep secret. As Clark goes through adolescence, he is ridiculed by some peers and mistrusted by neighbors because of his differences. When trapped in a storm, Jonathan refuses to let Clark rescue him, choosing to die rather than to expose Clark's powers.

After Jonathan dies, Clark travels the world seeking information about his birth family. Around this time, General Zod finds Earth. He learns that Jor-El has put the DNA information for all future Kryptonians into Kal-El's body. General Zod hopes to capture Kal-El, extract the information from him, destroy him, kill the Earthlings, and create a new Kryptonian society on the ruins of Earth.

The Adoption Connection

Clark was born far away but his birth parents decided that, for his own safety, they would send him to another world to be raised by other parents. He was adopted by the Kent family. Eventually, his adoptive father told him as much of his story as he knew. Clark is troubled after this and asks if he and the Kents can just keep pretending to be a family. Jonathan assures him that they are a family, and acknowledges that Clark also has another family. Jonathan encourages Clark to find out more about his story.

After Jonathan dies, Clark sets off to learn about his birth family. Clark also must decide whether he is a Kryptonian, a son of Earth, or both.

Clark stops keeping his powers completely secret, and instead begins sharing them with some very close friends. He has moved from Secrecy to Confidentiality.

Some kids who have experienced trauma prior to coming into foster care struggle with maintaining attention. They may relate to a scene in which a young Clark is overwhelmed by sensory input at school. Clark can see and hear more than the other kids, and he has to learn how to focus.

One character says that Clark has adopted humans, which mirrors the fact that humans adopted him.

Strong Points

Clark's birth parents made a painful but necessary choice when they sent him to Earth. We see their pain; they mourn the experiences with him that they will never have, but they still do what they believe is necessary for his safety. This element of Clark's story could help adoptees develop an understanding of how their birth families could have relinquished them while also loving them.

Clark's adoptive father shares the truth of Clark's story with him and acknowledges that Clark has another family and another name.

Clark is able to find an artificial intelligence based on his father, which allows him to learn about the history of his world and provides him with guidance. Clark is also able to ask why his birth parents did not come for him, and the answer is helpful to him: they could not come, but they loved him deeply. Jor-El encourages Clark to embody the best of Earth and the best of Krypton, rather than viewing himself as only a Kryptonian.

Clark's birth father and both of his adoptive parents encourage him to view both sides of his culture as good. This is particularly important because the Kryptonian criminals devalue Earth and the humans who know Clark mistrust him because of his abilities.

Challenges

Clark is encouraged to keep much of his identity hidden, because Jonathan feels that other people will not understand Clark if they know the whole truth about him. This is not the only film in which a character is told to keep their origins a secret for fear of what others might think—*The Odd Life of Timothy Green* is another that portrays this. Some real-life adoptions are governed by a similar code of secrecy, as families fear that people, including the adoptee, might not understand or accept their story. Fortunately, Clark is able to move from painful Secrecy into a workable Confidentiality.

At one point, Clark tells Jonathan that Jonathan is only someone who found him, but not his real father. Jonathan agrees with Clark, and Jonathan dies before he and Clark are able to revisit the conversation.

Jor-El is killed by General Zod in a violent fit of rage. Later, General Zod assaults Martha Kent.

Recommendations

Man of Steel seems most likely to appeal to teenagers and their parents. It could help viewers develop a sense of empathy for birth parents who have chosen to relinquish their children.

Clark's encounter with his birth father could let some viewers imagine what they would ask if they could contact a parent with whom they've lost contact.

Consider this one for teens of ages 13 and up.

Questions for Discussion

- Why did Jor-El and Lara send Clark to Earth? How did they feel about it?

- If you could talk with any relative that you've lost contact with, who would it be, and what would you talk about? What would you want to know? What would you want them to know?

- What parts of your story do you keep confidential? Which do you share openly? What do you think is the difference between Confidentiality and Secrecy?

- Martha said supportive things, but also seemed worried, when Clark told her that he found out about his birth family. Why was she worried?

- In what ways is Clark a son of Krypton? In what ways is he a son of Earth? In what ways is he uniquely himself?

- What parts of Clark's story remind you of yours?

- (For parents) How do you feel when you think of your children finding out about their birth families?

Secondhand Lions

(2003, PG, 111 minutes. Live Action. Starring Robert Duvall, Michael Caine, and Haley Joel Osment)

The Plot

Mae decides to leave her 14-year-old son, Walter, with his unsuspecting, elderly great-uncles Hub and Garth for the whole summer. This is not the first time Mae has left Walter for a long period of time and Walter does not believe that she always tells him the truth about her plans. Although they have never met Walter and barely know Mae, the uncles agree that Walter can stay.

Mae has suggested to Walter that Hub and Garth are rich. She lets Walter know that she hopes that Walter will be able to convince them to leave their money to him. Walter is not interested in the money but instead gets to know his ornery uncles.

His uncles take joy in shooting at travelling salesmen who are also trying to access their money but they do eventually buy a lion and let Walter keep it as a pet.

Walter learns from Garth that Hub and Garth shared amazing heroic adventures during a decades-long absence from their homeland. When Walter asks whether the stories are true, Hub replies that Walter's belief is more important than the actual truth of the stories.

Shortly after Walter has gotten comfortable with Garth and Hub, Mae shows up in the middle of the night with a new boyfriend. She tries to convince Walter to give her access to Hub's and Garth's money. When Walter does not comply her boyfriend beats Walter, but Walter's pet lion saves him.

Mae leaves with Walter and her boyfriend, but when Walter learns that she intends to live with her boyfriend, Walter asks for her blessing to return to Hub and Garth. She consents, and Walter returns to his great-uncles to be raised by them.

Years later, after Hub and Garth die, Walter learns that the great adventures of their stories were actually true.

The Adoption Connection

Walter was neglected by his mother. He was raised by his great-uncles temporarily but then asked to be raised by them permanently, and his mother consented. Many adoptions occur when a child is adopted by relatives. Although Hub and Garth do not appear to adopt Walter legally, they begin to function as his parents. As an adult, Walter reflects on his childhood and explains that Hub and Garth raised him.

Two elements of this film's adoption connection are relatively rare among other adoption-relevant movies: Walter's adoptive parents are his elderly relatives and Walter is raised by them because he asks his mother to let it happen.

Strong Points

Walter is able to tell his mother what he needs—to be raised by Hub and Garth—and she is able to listen to him. It is unfortunate that she does not seem to consider choosing her son over her violent boyfriend, but at least she lets Walter leave a dangerous situation.

This film presents a positive portrayal of a child being raised by relatives from an older generation than the child's parents. It also shows how an awkward, uncomfortable living situation when a child is first placed with a family can develop over time into a positive, nurturing home.

Challenges

Hub initially does not act warmly towards Walter, and the two old men shoot their guns at passing salesmen.

It might be hard for some viewers to see Walter mistreated by his dishonest, negligent mother and later physically abused by his mother's boyfriend. It seems that Mae's boyfriend may have also been abusive towards her, but she still intends to marry him.

We learn that Walter has spent time in an orphanage before, and it seems most likely that his mother abandoned him there for a time.

Another greedy relative threatens to send Walter to an orphanage. Walter runs away, but Garth and Hub find him and bring him back home.

Hub's adventures were true; he explains to Walter that he poured himself into heroic escapades because he did not know what else to do with himself after his wife and infant died during childbirth. This explanation is not graphic, mournful, or long, but it could be upsetting for some adult viewers who have unresolved grief around miscarriage or infertility issues.

One of Walter's great-uncles speaks negatively about Walter's mother, using rough language.

Recommendations

Secondhand Lions seems most likely to appeal to adults and some teenagers. It could be a helpful film for children ages 10 and up being adopted by older relatives or for teenagers who have finally entered an adoptive home after experiencing abuse, neglect, or a long time in foster care.

After watching it, consider talking about family narratives; listen to your teen's narratives about their family of origin and their time in other homes prior to coming to you, and offer some of your own personal interesting stories from your younger years.

Questions for Discussion

- What are your family's legendary stories?

- Why did Walter choose to live with Hub and Garth instead of with his mother?

- Would Hub's and Garth's stories have been less meaningful if they had turned out to be fiction?

Somewhere Between

(2011, Not rated, 88 minutes. Documentary.
Directed by Linda Goldstein Knowlton)

The Plot

Filmmaker Linda Goldstein Knowlton adopted her daughter Ruby from China, but knows that Ruby will have many questions about her own identity that Linda will not be able to answer.

Linda proactively creates this documentary for her daughter; she gets to know four teenage girls who were adopted into the US from China and follows them as they learn more about their own identities.

One teen meets her birth family for the first time and learns about the circumstances of her placement. Another tries to find out what her specific ethnic heritage might be. One teen returns to China and finds a young girl in a foster home who is thought to be hopeless because of cerebral palsy. The young girl receives rehabilitative services, proudly shares her newfound abilities, and ultimately meets a family that has been longing to adopt her.

The Adoption Connection

Somewhere Between is about adoption and it was filmed because of adoption—Knowlton made the film for Ruby. It thoroughly explores the feelings involved in reconnecting with birth family members and provides insight into identity formation in teenagers who have been adopted internationally.

The film also briefly addresses a Chinese policy that made some families desire to have only one child.

Strong Points

The filmmaker is aware that a child adopted internationally will have questions about their heritage and history and has worked proactively to prepare answers to those eventual questions from her daughter.

The teens are open and insightful with their stories. They seem to find it helpful to know others who have had similar experiences.

A teenager who was relinquished to an orphanage without her birth father knowing is excitedly welcomed back to the village of her birth family with a huge celebration. Her adoptive family and birth family share a homemade meal and a heartwarming, loving, and emotional visit. The teenager's father, who had not been able to name her as an infant, gives her a Chinese name that honors her as a person having two families. The teen finds this very meaningful. It is sad when it is time for her to leave the village, but her father asks her to come back to visit again.

Challenges

One child remembers the day when she was abandoned by a relative. She has developed into a remarkably successful and kind young adult, and she seems to have made peace with her story. Some young viewers might find the story hard to hear if it comes close to their own unprocessed grief.

Abandonment language is used by teens and adults in the film, which could also be hard for some viewers.

The teens meet one man who believes international adoption should not happen. He encourages one of them to find her birth family as soon as possible, since records are often lost.

Recommendations

There is a lot of good content in this film. The teens share their thoughts, stories, journeys, and insecurities, and in doing so they have helped to create a profoundly insightful and worthwhile documentary.

Somewhere Between should be helpful and interesting to prospective adoptive families, as well as teenagers who have been adopted.

Questions for Discussion

- If you never knew your birth parents, would you want to find them?

- A couple of the teens described themselves as looking Asian but feeling white "on the inside." What do you think of what they said? Do you think they feel pressure to say that they feel they fit in, or do you think it's actually how they feel?

- One teen suggests that a higher power is involved in adoption; what do you think? Do you believe that some higher power played a role in your adoption?

- Do you ever feel mad at your birth parents?

- How did belonging to a group of other adopted teens help these teens?

- One teen expresses that she is reluctant to find her birth mother, even though she wants to, because she does not want to make either her birth mother or her adoptive mother feel uncomfortable. Can you relate? Why does she worry about that? Would it be fair of her mothers to expect her to worry about that? What might help her feel less worried?

- What are some ways that adoption affects your life?

- Do you ever feel like you are stuck between two cultures?

- One teen expressed how important it is to her to find people who look like her. Is that important to you at this point in your life?

- Can a person be—at the same time—happy with their adoptive family and desirous of finding their birth family?

- Are there any words you wish weren't used when people talk about adoption?

- Are there any questions you have about your adoption story or history?

- How do you imagine that your birth family feels about you?

- One teen describes what her ideal world would be like and then acknowledges that there is no ideal world but that we have to live in the world we get. If you could design your ideal world, with regard to all of your family, what would it look like?

- (For parents) Whose responsibility should it be to bring up questions of culture and birth family?

Star Wars: Episode I: The Phantom Menace

(1999, PG, 133 minutes. Live Action. Starring Liam Neeson,
Ewan McGregor, Natalie Portman, and Jake Lloyd)

The Plot

The Trade Federation has created a blockade of ships around the planet Naboo. The galactic peacekeepers called Jedi have sent two representatives, Qui-Gon Jinn and Obi-Wan Kenobi, to negotiate an end to the blockade.

Unbeknownst to them, the Trade Federation is under the advisement of a Sith Lord. The Sith are the antithesis of the Jedi. Both tap into a universal life force, but while the Jedi are selfless, the Sith are driven by personal ambition and tap into the Dark Side of the Force. The Sith Lord advises the Trade Federation to kill the Jedi.

The Jedi manage to escape along with Naboo's teenage Queen Amidala, but damage to their ship requires them to stop for repairs on the desert planet of Tatooine. There, they meet nine-year-old Anakin Skywalker, a slave in whom Qui-Gon senses a strong connection to the Force. Qui-Gon believes that Anakin is intended to fulfill a prophecy about bringing the Force into balance.

Qui-Gon wins Anakin's freedom in a game of chance and intends to take Anakin away from Tatooine in order to train him and develop his potential as a Jedi. Qui-Gon is mortally wounded by an adversary and so asks his apprentice, Obi-Wan, to train Anakin in his stead.

The Adoption Connection

Anakin only knows his mother; she says that Anakin was born of the Force, and that there was no father. Anakin must choose to leave his mother in order to train to be a Jedi, although he promises to come back to rescue her.

Qui-Gon and, later, Obi-Wan develop a master–apprentice relationship with Anakin, which is at least somewhat familial.

Some kids—perhaps those who have been adopted into one home after having a positive foster care experience in another—will resonate with Anakin's experience of being transferred from one nurturing parent figure to another. In Anakin's case, he voluntarily leaves his mother. Anakin's choice in leaving his mother will be atypical of many viewers' own experiences.

Some adoption stories will resemble the fact that Anakin leaves a very difficult situation, with the blessing of his mother, in the hope of finding a better life far away with other caretakers.

Strong Points

The *Star Wars* saga is, in many ways, the story of Anakin Skywalker. Although he will later become known under another name, here we see his roots—as the loved son of a caring mother.

Challenges

Anakin and his mother are slaves and his mother is not able to prevent Anakin's owner from subjecting him to dangerous activities. She explains that it pains her deeply each time it happens.

Some viewers might find it hard to see Anakin choose to leave his mother, his friends, and his home-world, even though he intends to come back eventually to make things better for his mother. He asks whether he'll ever see her again, and neither he nor his mother are able to give a definite answer to the question.

One Jedi Master tells Anakin, in a roundabout way, that fear of losing his mother can lead to hate and suffering. It might be true, but it does not make room for Anakin's real and understandable feelings of sadness at leaving his mother. Young viewers who mourn the loss of a parent might find this Jedi Master's advice unhelpful.

Nine-year-old Anakin takes responsibility for his mom's safety. Some kids who have been neglected prior to entering foster care feel an adult-level sense of responsibility for their siblings and even their parents; Anakin's resolve might resonate with them, even if it is unfair for Anakin to feel responsible for his mom.

The death and subsequent funeral pyre of a Jedi might be disturbing to some young viewers.

Recommendations

The Phantom Menace introduces Anakin Skywalker as a nine-year-old boy who leaves a difficult life for the potential of a better life far from where he was born.

The *Star Wars* series follows Anakin's story and the stories of his children. On its own, this movie is a story about Anakin leaving one family and acclimating to another sort of family, but it is best viewed as the first of six movies that together tell a story of loss, identity formation, and multiple instances of family reunification. There are many adoption themes throughout the series to explore with your kids.

This film, and most of the series in general, seems best suited to kids of ages 10 and up and their parents.

Questions for Discussion

- What range of feelings did Anakin have as he left Tatooine?

- What range of feelings might Anakin's mom have had when Anakin chose to leave Tatooine to become a Jedi?

- What do you think it would have been like to drive a Pod Racer?

- Why were the Jedi scared to train Anakin? Do you think they were right or wrong to be so reluctant to train him?

Star Wars: Episode II: Attack of the Clones

(2002, PG, 142 minutes. Live Action. Starring Ewan McGregor, Natalie Portman, Hayden Christensen, Samuel L. Jackson, Ian McDiarmid, and Christopher Lee)

The Plot

Ten years after the events of *The Phantom Menace*, Anakin Skywalker is a teenage prodigy, still under the tutelage of Obi-Wan Kenobi.

When Senator Padmé Amidala (formerly Queen Amidala) arrives at Coruscant to cast a vote against a separatist movement she narrowly avoids two assassination attempts. The Jedi send Obi-Wan to attempt to discover the identity of those trying to kill Padmé while Anakin is assigned to take Padmé back to her home planet and keep her safe.

While hunting down Padmé's secret enemy, Obi-Wan discovers that an army is being secretly constructed for the Galactic Republic. The army is comprised of clones of a bounty hunter named Jango Fett. Obi Wan tracks Jango and his young son to a desert world where Obi-Wan is captured.

Anakin and Padmé have left Padmé's home planet of Naboo in response to a premonition Anakin had about his mother suffering. Anakin finds his mother, but she has been tortured by kidnappers and she dies just after Anakin finds her. In a fit of rage, Anakin slays all people in the community where he found his mother. He confesses this to Padmé, then buries his mother at the homestead of the Lars family, into which she had recently married.

Anakin and Padmé receive a message showing that Obi-Wan is in distress. They set off to rescue him against overwhelming odds.

Meanwhile, the Sith Lord Darth Sidious continues to manipulate the events of the galaxy while working himself into a position of advantage.

Anakin and Padmé have fallen in love, and after completing their rescue mission, they secretly marry.

The Adoption Connection

After leaving his mother and his home-world at nine years of age, Anakin has been raised by Jedi. He remembers the promise that he made his mother when he left—that he would return to free her from slavery.

When he has a troubling vision, he returns to his home-world to save her, but finds that she has been kidnapped and tortured. She dies in his arms, making permanent a loss that Anakin had expected to be temporary. Anakin's grief at his loss causes him to act out violently.

Later, Anakin expresses that he blames himself for the loss of his mother; he pledges to do whatever it takes to ensure that he never experiences the loss of another loved one.

Anakin is not the only character to experience the traumatic death of a parent; Jango Fett dies while his young son Boba looks on helplessly.

Anakin had no father and the Republic has created an army of clones who have no mother. Jango Fett has claimed one of the clones as his son and has raised him for several years.

Strong Points

When Anakin blames himself for the death of his mother, Padmé tries to comfort him by saying that it was not his responsibility because no one can fix everything.

When Anakin sees his mother before she dies, she communicates that she loves him.

Challenges

When Anakin finds his mother, she is bound and wounded. She shares a few brief words with Anakin before dying in his arms. Although she is at peace, he is in torment. It could be a hard scene for young viewers.

Young Boba Fett sees his villainous father decapitated in a battle. He holds his father's helmet to his own head in a moment of mourning.

Recommendations

Some people who have been adopted—perhaps especially those adopted from foster care—may feel as though they are responsible for the circumstances that led to their adoption. Anakin blames himself for not preventing the death of his mother. In neither case is the blame healthy. As you watch this film, consider the role of false blame in the lives of those who have lost connections with loved ones. As you continue through the *Star Wars* movies, notice how Anakin's reaction to this painful loss shapes his approach to life.

Like most of the other *Star Wars* films, *Attack of the Clones* seems best suited to kids of ages 10 and up and their parents, although the scene in which Anakin finds his mother might be hard for the younger kids in this age group.

Questions for Discussion

- Anakin blamed himself for not being able to save his mother; was his blame fairly placed?

- Anakin is hurting, and he wants to ensure that no one he loves will ever die again. Is his goal possible? Can you think of a better goal for him?

- Have you ever blamed yourself for something that really wasn't your fault?

- Is there anyone who you miss? How do you feel about missing them? How do you deal with those feelings?

Star Wars: Episode III: Revenge of the Sith

(2005, PG-13, 140 minutes. Live Action. Starring Ewan
McGregor, Natalie Portman, and Hayden Christensen)

The Plot

Anakin Skywalker and Obi-Wan Kenobi continue to
represent the Jedi as they try to help the Galactic Senate
fend off threats from a separatist movement. They save the
Supreme Chancellor Palpatine and kill two of the leaders of
the separatists.

Anakin also learns that his secret wife, Padmé, is
pregnant. Anakin is initially excited, but begins having
visions of Padmé dying during childbirth. Previously,
Anakin had visions of his mother suffering, and those came
true. He is desperate to find a way to prevent Padmé's death.
Sensing this, Palpatine confides to Anakin that Palpatine
understands the Dark Side of the Force and promises that
he can help Anakin stop Padmé from dying. Anakin initially
refuses to follow Palpatine's evil ways but eventually gives in.

Palpatine takes Anakin as a Sith apprentice and renames
him Darth Vader. His first order is for Vader to participate in
an effort to kill all of the Jedi. Out of a fear of losing Padmé,
Anakin betrays the Jedi, and starts by slaughtering everyone
at the Jedi temple, including all the children in training.

When Padmé learns of this, she begs Anakin to return
to her, but she has also brought Obi-Wan Kenobi with her.
Anakin is enraged, believing that she has betrayed him. He
uses the Force to choke her into unconsciousness and begins
to battle his former master, Obi-Wan. Obi-Wan wins the
fight, severing Anakin's limbs and leaving Anakin for dead.

Obi-Wan escapes with Padmé while Palpatine, who has declared himself Emperor of the Galactic Empire, collects Anakin. Obi-Wan takes Padmé to a secret place where she gives birth to twins whom she names Luke and Leia. Padmé then dies.

Obi-Wan and others decide that, for the safety of the children, they must be hidden from the Emperor and from their father Anakin, who has now become the evil Darth Vader. Luke is taken to live with his grandmother's husband's son's family on Tatooine, and Leia is adopted by a senator and his wife, who live on another world. Leia's new father shares that he and his wife have always considered adopting.

Meanwhile, the Emperor crafts a new armored suit to allow Anakin to live as Darth Vader, but tells Vader that, in a fit of rage, Vader himself killed Padmé.

The Adoption Connection

Revenge of the Sith continues the story of Anakin Skywalker. Anakin left his mother in the first film, and watched her die in the second. Now, his wife has died, and he is unaware that his children survived. His children will be raised in secrecy, outside of his knowledge and away from his dangerous involvement with the evil Emperor. They will be raised separately from each other, and without knowledge of each other.

Anakin's rage all flows from his grief and anger at the loss of his mother and his fear of the loss of Padmé.

Strong Points

Although their history is tragic, Luke and Leia have people who will love and support them.

It would be easy for people to consider Darth Vader a pure villain but the first three movies let us see his fears and hopes and the way that he was manipulated by the evil Palpatine. Most behaviors make sense within a certain context, and if we understand the context of those behaviors we are less likely to vilify even the people of whom we are afraid. This could be a helpful skill for foster parents whose children have birth parents who have a history of violence or abuse. It might be reasonable to be afraid and cautious around them, but it is not helpful to vilify them. Seeing the humanity of your child's birth parents can help you help your child avoid a one-sided view of their birth parents, which in turn can help them have a healthier view of themselves.

Challenges

This film struck me as more violent than the other *Star Wars* films; Anakin's limbs are cut off and he is burned by lava. Anakin decapitates a helpless foe. Although it is not shown on film, Anakin slays a room full of children.

Yoda wisely tells Anakin that death is a natural part of life. However, he also tells Anakin that attachment can develop into jealousy, and he advises Anakin to be detached. Better advice would be to accept that loss and pain are inevitable, but still to attach to those you love.

Recommendations

Unlike the rest of the *Star Wars* films, *Revenge of the Sith* is a bit more violent, and might be best reserved for kids of ages 13 and up and their parents.

As you watch it, notice how loss and the fear of more loss affected Anakin's behaviors and left him vulnerable to manipulation. Also, imagine how you might describe Anakin if you were called upon to raise Luke or Leia.

Questions for Discussion

- What caused Anakin to respond so negatively to the losses he experienced?

- Was it important for Luke and Leia to be kept secret from Darth Vader?

- Was it important for Luke and Leia to be kept secret from each other?

- How can we experience loss without being consumed by it?

- If you were raising Luke or Leia, how would you explain their birth father to them? Can you find an honest way to explain him that does not paint him as purely evil?

Star Wars: Episode IV: A New Hope

(1977, PG, 121 minutes. Live Action. Starring Mark Hamill, Harrison Ford, and Carrie Fisher)

The Plot

Almost two decades ago, Obi-Wan Kenobi made the hard decision to hide Anakin Skywalker's twin children from him and, as a result, the children are also unknown to each other. Anakin is now the feared Sith lord Darth Vader, and he is unaware that his children are alive.

Luke Skywalker, who still bears his father's original last name, is living with an aunt and an uncle on the desert planet

Tatooine. Luke is fascinated by news of the Rebellion being led against the evil Galactic Empire.

Luke accidentally intercepts a message from Leia, which leads him into the desert where he meets Obi-Wan, who has been keeping tabs on him. Obi-Wan invites Luke to train to be a Jedi, and when Luke discovers that the Empire has killed his aunt and uncle, he agrees to be trained.

Like his father, Luke is a gifted pilot, and is strong in the Force. Obi-Wan gives Luke his father's lightsaber but does not tell Luke that his father has become the evil Darth Vader; instead, he says that Darth Vader killed Luke's father.

Luke and Obi-Wan hire the smuggler Han Solo to transport them to the planet of Alderaan to deliver a message vital to the Rebellion, but the Empire has already destroyed the planet with a new powerful weapon. Instead, they rescue Leia.

Luke and his new friends must attempt to destroy the Empire's weapon while Obi-Wan must face Darth Vader for the first time since their battle nearly 20 years prior.

The Adoption Connection

Luke Skywalker knows very little of his father. He begins to learn about Anakin—and about being a Jedi—from Obi-Wan, but the information that Obi-Wan gives Luke seems to be inaccurate.

One of the leaders of the Rebellion is Leia Organa. Luke thinks she is beautiful and attempts to save her from the Empire, which has captured her and sentenced her to death. Unbeknownst to either of them, Leia is Luke's twin sister. Leia is imprisoned by Darth Vader, who does not realize that she is his daughter.

Strong Points

Although it is initially influenced by misinformation, Luke develops a balanced and positive view of his father throughout this trilogy instead of focusing only on his father's very obvious faults. It will be a long road, but this film sets the scene for a future film in which Luke will prove that there is still good in Anakin Skywalker.

Even though Luke has never met his father, he shares gifts and mannerisms with him and even follows in his footsteps to some degree.

Challenges

Luke's aunt and uncle withhold information from him—and his uncle lies to him—about Obi-Wan and Anakin. They hope to keep him from turning out like his father. Later, Obi-Wan misleads Luke about his father, as well. All the misinformation is intended for Luke's benefit, but it would be easy to imagine him feeling betrayed.

Luke finds the burning corpses of his aunt and uncle after the Empire kills them.

Luke's relatives suggest that Luke is too similar to his father for his own good.

Luke sees Darth Vader appear to kill Obi-Wan. This is another traumatic loss for Luke, who grew up without a father, never knew his mother, and just recently saw the burning bodies of the aunt and uncle who raised him. The way that Luke responds to loss is quite different from the way Anakin responded to loss; people can respond differently to similar situations.

Recommendations

A New Hope continues the story of Anakin Skywalker while shifting the focus to his son.

This film seems best suited to kids of ages 10 and up, and their parents.

As you watch it, think about the motivations the characters had for keeping secrets from Luke and how they might have handled the information differently.

Questions for Discussion

- What does Luke believe about his father? Which parts of his beliefs are true? Which parts are false?

- Why have Luke's aunt and uncle kept information from him? Do you agree with them?

- If you could be any character from the movie, who would you be? Which character would you want to have as a friend?

Star Wars: Episode V: The Empire Strikes Back

(1980, PG, 124 minutes. Live Action. Starring Mark Hamill, Harrison Ford, Carrie Fisher, and Billy Dee Williams)

The Plot

Three years after Luke destroyed the Empire's Death Star, the Empire has found the hidden Rebel base. Luke, Han Solo, and Leia all escape the base.

Luke goes to the swamp planet Dagobah to train as a Jedi under Yoda, an ancient Jedi Master who has trained many other Jedi.

Han and Leia attempt to hide from the Empire with one of Han's friends but Han is betrayed and turned over to a bounty hunter.

Leia is captured by Darth Vader, who intends to use her as bait to draw out Luke. Vader believes that Luke is his son and Vader's Sith Master, the Emperor Palpatine, has commanded Vader to bring Luke to the Emperor to be trained as another Sith.

The Adoption Connection

While in training with Yoda, Luke has a vision in which his own face is hidden under Darth Vader's helmet. This seems to imply that Luke already senses on some level that there is a connection between him and Darth Vader.

Darth Vader reveals to Luke that he is Luke's father, and Luke screams in horror at the revelation. Luke and Darth Vader have a lightsaber duel.

Like others before, Yoda notices important similarities between Luke and his father.

Because they are siblings, Luke is able to call telepathically to Leia.

Strong Points

Luke and Leia have a strong sibling bond, even though they have not yet realized that they are siblings.

Even though Obi-Wan has died, Luke still relies on him for guidance. It might be helpful for some viewers to see that even though someone has been lost, memories of that person can still serve for guidance, direction, and wisdom.

Challenges

Leia kisses Luke on the mouth to provoke jealousy in another man; neither she nor Luke realize that they are siblings.

Darth Vader invites Luke to join him in his evil work. He also cuts off Luke's hand.

Han keeps Luke warm by slicing open a recently deceased animal and putting Luke inside. It was necessary to do this to keep Luke alive in the freezing temperatures, but seeing the beast's innards pour out is a bit gross.

Recommendations

Like most of the other *Star Wars* films, *The Empire Strikes Back* seems best suited for kids of ages 10 and up and their parents.

As Luke learns that Darth Vader is his father, viewers can explore the ways that Luke is like his father and the ways that he is different from his father.

Families can use this film to start conversations about the people and thoughts that are formative in their kids' lives.

Questions for Discussion

- In what ways is Luke like his father? In what ways is he different?

- In what ways are you like your birth parents? In what ways are you different from them?

- What do you think of the advice Yoda gives to Luke? What parts do you agree with? What parts do you disagree with?

- Luke was guided by Obi-Wan, even though Obi-Wan has died. How can people that we do not see still influence or guide us? Who influences or guides you?

- Do you ever wonder if you might be around relatives without knowing it? What do you think about it?

Star Wars: Episode VI: Return of the Jedi

(1983, PG, 131 minutes. Live Action. Starring Mark Hamill, Harrison Ford, Carrie Fisher, and Billy Dee Williams)

The Plot

Luke, Leia, and their friends set off to rescue Han Solo, who has been captured by a bounty hunter and turned over to a crime lord.

After rescuing Han, many of their group join the Rebel effort to destroy the Empire's new Death Star, but Luke first travels back to Dagobah to complete his training with Yoda. Although Yoda is near death, he confirms that Darth Vader is Luke's father.

Obi-Wan Kenobi appears and helps Luke realize that Leia is his sister.

Luke learns that he must confront Darth Vader and is cautioned to avoid turning to the Dark Side of the Force. Luke turns himself over to the Empire and tries to convince his father to turn away from the Dark Side, saying that there is still good in him. His father refuses, and brings Luke to his Sith Master, Emperor Palpatine.

Palpatine encourages Luke and his father to battle each other. They fight but Luke refuses to kill Vader, even after Vader suggests that Luke's sister could be turned to the Dark Side.

The Emperor attempts to kill Luke, but Darth Vader saves Luke and kills the Emperor. Darth Vader is mortally wounded, but he asks to be unmasked before he dies. Now, as Anakin Skywalker, he sees Luke face to face and dies at peace.

The Adoption Connection

Luke receives confirmation from Yoda that Darth Vader is his father, Anakin Skywalker. Luke confronts his father. He discovers that his friend Leia is his sister.

Luke and his father are on opposite sides of a war, and each tries to persuade the other to change sides.

Luke maintains a belief that his father has goodness in him, and eventually he is proved right. Luke and Anakin are reconciled to each other before Anakin dies.

Luke and Leia discuss their birth mother. Leia has some memories of her; Luke has none.

Luke and Leia each perceived their sibling relationship before it was revealed to them.

Strong Points

Although the Emperor anticipates that Luke's compassionate understanding of his father will be a weakness, Luke's hopefulness is ultimately justified.

Anakin Skywalker turned to the Dark Side in an unsuccessful attempt to prevent the death of a loved member of his family. Now he prevents the death of his son by turning away from the Dark Side.

Luke has learned difficult information about his birth family that others have tried to hide from him out of fear that he would be harmed by the truth. However, Luke handles the knowledge very well and is able to achieve reconciliation with his father and peace with his own identity.

Challenges

Yoda seems surprised that Luke knows that Darth Vader is his father. Luke initially believes that Yoda is upset that Luke has discovered the truth of his parentage, but Yoda replies that he only regrets that Luke found out before Yoda thought he was ready.

Luke confronts Obi-Wan, who had told Luke that Darth Vader killed his father; Obi-Wan gives an unsatisfying answer that what he had said could be seen as true, in some ways. It would be understandable if Luke felt that he had been lied to.

Obi-Wan expresses that Luke's refusal to kill his father amounts to defeat, but he is proved wrong. Obi-Wan also tells Luke to hide his feelings.

When referring to Padmé, Luke's word choice might be taken to imply that his Aunt Beru, who adopted him, is not really his mother.

Luke and Darth Vader have an epic lightsaber battle; Luke cuts off his father's hand, much as his father cut off Luke's hand in a previous fight. In this moment, Luke appears to see similarities between himself and his father, and this realization helps Luke resist the Emperor's influence.

Luke sees his father die, but it is peaceful. Luke gives him a proper Jedi funeral by burning his body on a pyre.

Recommendations

Return of the Jedi concludes the story of Anakin Skywalker. He has found healing and has been reconciled with his son. Luke has learned and successfully handled difficult truths about his birth family that others had wanted to hide from him.

This film seems likely to be a good fit for kids of ages 10 and up and their parents.

After watching it, think about talking with your kids about a nuanced view of their birth family, using the film to convey that it is OK to believe that there is goodness in everyone.

Also, consider the way that Luke dealt with information that others, trying to act in his best interest, had wanted to keep from him. Consider how your family handles the difficult aspects of your children's adoption story.

Questions for Discussion

- How do you feel about how Obi-Wan, and later Yoda, handled the truth of Darth Vader being Luke's father?

- How do you think Luke felt when he learned that Leia was his sister?

- Do you ever wonder whether you have siblings who you have not met or think about siblings who you have lost touch with?

- Luke persevered in his belief that good remained in his father, and he was right. Have you ever believed that there was good in someone, even though it would have been easy to vilify them? Tell me about that.

- Which aspects of your birth family are you unhappy about? From which aspects of your birth family can you draw good traits and good feelings?

Star Wars: Episode VII: The Force Awakens

(2015, PG-13, 136 minutes. Live Action. Starring
Mark Hamill, Harrison Ford, Carrie Fisher, John
Boyega, Daisy Ridley, and Adam Driver)

The Plot

Thirty years after the destruction of the Death Star in *Return of the Jedi*, the First Order rises from the ashes of the evil Empire and tries to destroy the New Republic. The First Order believe that to ensure victory they must find and destroy Luke Skywalker, who they believe to be the last Jedi.

The New Republic also desire to find Skywalker. They believe that he will guide them to victory, much as the Jedis were instrumental in defeating the Empire 30 years ago.

As both sides race to find him, Finn, a conscience-stricken First Order soldier, runs away from his army and teams up with an undiscovered prodigy named Rey.

The Adoption Connection

Themes of family run strong in this one. Two characters hope to find long-missing relatives. Rey leaves her home in a quest to do good, but longs to return because she still hopes to be reunited with her long-lost loved ones. Leia's brother Luke went into exile after one of his students went rogue and she hopes to find him. Kylo Ren has renounced the teachings of his parents and embraces the former lifestyle of his deceased grandfather Darth Vader. Han Solo and Leia have a child together, but their relationship has become strained and their son is estranged from them.

A few characters comment that a person's lineage determines the paths that they are prone to follow in life.

It seems to be suggested that this holds true even if there is not a relationship between members of different generations of a family. A character is told that he cannot deny his family's influence.

The First Order fills its ranks by abducting children from their families; an adult explains that he will never know his family.

Strong Points

The film highlights the fact that we do not want to forget those we love, even when they are absent from us.

One character advises Rey that, instead of returning to her past relationships, she needs to embrace her future to find where she belongs. It might have been more accurate to have advised her that she can find belonging and meaning in her past, but also in her present and her future.

Challenges

The scenes and themes of forceful governmental abduction of children could be traumatic for kids who remember being removed from their parents.

Scenes of fire and gunfire and scenes of Kylo Ren's unpredictable and explosive temper could be scary to kids who have experienced violence.

Kylo Ren is conflicted between the good that his parents have taught him and the evil that he believes also runs in his family. He is confronted by his father, who hopes to repair the relationship. Although Kylo Ren appears ready to reconcile with his father, he murders him instead. This scene could be traumatic for viewers who are estranged from their birth parents or other parental figures; it could also be painful for parents who are separated from their children.

Recommendations

The Force Awakens is likely to appeal to kids, teens, and adults. Kylo Ren's murder of his father and themes of a family torn apart could be difficult for some viewers.

This one seems best geared towards kids of ages 10 and up, with parents in the room to talk about the movie afterwards and to make sure that the scenes of violence aren't making too big an impact.

As you watch it, think about talking about the way that birth family and adoptive family history can influence your child's life.

Questions for Discussion

- In which ways does your lineage define you and your path in life? In which ways does it not define you?

- Does your sense of belonging lie behind you, ahead of you, or both? In what ways is it something you find? In what ways is it something you create?

- For parents, how important is it to you that your children follow in your footsteps? Which aspects are most important to you? Which are less important to you? Which are unimportant to you?

Superman: The Movie

(1978, PG, 143 minutes. Live Action. Starring Christopher
Reeve, Marlon Brando, Gene Hackman, and Margot Kidder)

The Plot

Jor-El believes that the planet Krypton is about to explode.
Although he is unable to convince the other leaders of the
planet to vacate, he and his wife Lara manage to send their
infant son Kal-El on a journey to Earth. Shortly after Kal-
El's shuttle leaves, Krypton is destroyed.

During Kal-El's three-year journey, he is educated by
messages that his father left for him.

Kal-El lands on Earth as a three-year-old child. He
is discovered and adopted by Jonathan and Martha Kent,
who live in a small town in Kansas. The boy, who they name
Clark, has superhuman powers that the Kents advise him to
keep hidden, fearing how others will react.

When Clark is 18, Jonathan dies. Clark is telepathically
drawn to a meeting with an image of Jor-El, who instructs
him about his heritage and tells him to serve the Earth.

After 12 years of training with Jor-El, Clark returns
and begins a double life as a mild-mannered newspaper
reporter named Clark Kent and the famous caped superhero,
Superman. He is just in time, since the evil Lex Luthor
intends to divert a nuclear missile to California.

The Adoption Connection

Kal-El is sent away by his birth parents because they believe
that they will not be able to keep him safe. He is adopted,
raised, loved, and named by the Kent family.

As a young adult, he learns about his Kryptonian heritage and incorporates it into his identity. When he finally meets his birth father, the first thing Kal-El asks about is his own identity.

Strong Points

Even though Jor-El is not physically with his son, he sends his memories with his son in order to instruct and guide him. He promises that his son will never be alone, and declares that his son will always carry his father within him.

Jor-El encourages his son to live as a human but always to be proud of his Kryptonian heritage.

Challenges

Jor-El selflessly sends Kal-El away to safety; but perhaps the separation was not necessary. Jor-El speaks for himself and Lara, and promises that neither he nor Lara will leave the planet. He makes this promise to appease the leadership of the planet, who do not believe that it is in danger. I find myself wondering why he made and kept that promise; he could have left Krypton and been present throughout his son's life.

Martha Kent expresses that she has prayed for a child. She is overjoyed to find Clark, but she does not seem interested in finding out about his birth family. She suggests to her husband that they could fabricate a story about how he came to their family.

When Clark declares that he has to leave, Martha expresses that she has always known that he would have to leave one day.

We see Jonathan drop dead of a heart attack.

Recommendations

Superman: The Movie is a classic film that should be fun for most kids of ages 7–15, as long as they are not too scared by Jonathan's death.

Afterwards, parents can use the film to have discussions about multifaceted identity.

The film also provides an understandable depiction of how a birth parent's decision to send their child away might be selfless, in the child's best interest, and motivated by love for the child. Seeing Jor-El and Lara grieve as they send Superman away could be helpful for kids who struggle to understand how a parent could relinquish a child they love.

Questions for Discussion

- Is Superman's real name Kal-El or Clark Kent, or are they both his real names?

- Why did Jor-El and Lara send their son away? Why didn't they go with him? How do you think they felt about what they had to do?

- If you could meet with your birth parents and ask them anything, which questions would you want to ask?

- If you could have any two of Superman's powers, which would you want?

Chapter 8

MOVIES FOR PARENTS

It's important for parents to practice self-care and for people who are co-parenting to nourish their relationship. Watching enjoyable films can accomplish both of those goals, and the films in this section can also allow for interesting and meaningful adult conversations about adoption. While some of the movies suggested here might be enjoyable for some kids, they seem most likely to appeal to adults and the questions are geared towards parents. Grab a movie and enjoy some stimulating, thoughtful conversation.

The questions in this section explore your journey towards adoption, including your motivation, insecurities, and unmet expectations. The questions also look at your hopes for parenting and the impact you want to make on your kids. Other questions are geared towards understanding and helpfully responding to your kids' behaviors. More questions explore birth family issues: how you think about birth family members, how you feel about your kids' thoughts about birth family members, and the relationships that you and your kids might have with their birth family. Questions in this section also address confidentiality and the importance of being intentional with the language that is used about adoption and about kids.

Antwone Fisher

(2002, PG-13, 120 minutes. Live Action. Written by Antwone
Fisher, and starring Denzel Washington and Derek Luke)

The Plot

Antwone Fisher never met his father and never knew his
mother. After being born in jail, Antwone was placed in
foster care. His mother never came to claim him.

Antwone was eventually thrown out of his foster home
after enduring years of physical, psychological, and sexual
abuse.

After a return to an orphanage and a subsequent period
of homelessness, Antwone enlists in the Navy. After a
fight with a superior officer, Antwone is required to attend
counseling. His therapist Dr. Davenport helps him explore
his history and convinces Antwone that he needs to find his
birth family in order to find closure.

With the help of his new love, a fellow Navy sailor named
Cheryl, Antwone goes on leave to try to find the family he
has never known. He is able to meet and forgive his mother
for never coming to get him. Then, he is surprised to be fully
embraced by the extended family of his late father.

The Adoption Connection

Antwone was raised in an abusive foster home and was never
adopted. As an adult, lingering effects from his childhood
are affecting his functioning, and he must reconnect with
his past to get closure in order to be able to function in
the future.

Antwone's reaction to perceived abandonment is very strong and it colors his relationship with his therapist on a few occasions.

Strong Points

As an adult, Antwone confronts those who have abused him and tells them that they did not destroy him. He finds his mother, expresses his deep feelings to her, and forgives her for not coming to get him. He and his girlfriend are fully embraced by his father's family who welcome him with a banquet just like the family banquets he has dreamed about.

Dr. Davenport discovers the unconscious processes that drive some of Antwone's behaviors. To those who do not know Antwone, he might seem unpredictably explosive, but the film can be used to illustrate that most behaviors do make sense within a certain context.

Antwone writes a powerful poem to express his inward grief and he reads the poem to his therapist.

Antwone's therapist is a caring, competent professional.

Challenges

Antwone has experienced loss. Antwone's father was killed by an ex-girlfriend. Antwone is present when his best friend is killed attempting to rob a store at gunpoint.

It is difficult to see and hear some of the abuse that Antwone experiences in his foster home; his foster mother regularly uses racial slurs, whips him with a wet towel, handcuffs him, and threatens him with fire. His foster aunt sexually molests him. His foster mother tells him that his mother is no good and does not want him.

At a Thanksgiving meal, a stranger asks Antwone prying questions about his family. Antwone becomes uncomfortable and leaves the table.

Recommendations

Like *Closure*, this is a film about someone travelling far to connect with their unknown birth family. *Antwone Fisher* is an emotional journey of self-exploration and healing.

It seems likely to be helpful to adoptive parents who want to hone their understanding and empathy for what their teens might be feeling. It might also be helpful for young adults on similar journeys of self-discovery.

Questions for Discussion

- Which behaviors have you seen in yourself or in your teenagers that initially didn't make sense to you? From which perspective did they make sense?

- Why is it important for Antwone to find his birth family? His visit with his mother wasn't the joyful reunion he might have hoped for; why was it still valuable?

- How was therapy helpful to Antwone? In what ways does Dr. Davenport differ from your experiences or expectations of a therapist?

- If you had never met one of your parents, what would you want to know from them?

- If you wrote a poem about some of the hard parts of your life experience, how would it go?

Belle

(2013, PG, 104 minutes. Live Action. Starring Gugu
Mbatha-Raw, Tom Wilkinson, and Sarah Gadon)

The Plot

In late 18th-century England, Dido is the daughter of a
British Royal Navy officer and an enslaved woman. After
her mother dies, her father comes and brings her to live with
his relatives.

While he is away at sea for many years, Dido is raised
by her paternal great-aunt and great-uncle. Dido's great-
uncle is the Lord Chief Justice, and he is preparing to make
a ruling regarding slave trade. Some members of high society
question his ability to rule justly because he has come to love
his biracial grand-niece as a daughter.

Dido and her white cousin Elizabeth live as sisters for
many years and both come into adulthood as the Lord Chief
Justice is nearing his court decision. Each hopes to marry,
however Elizabeth is mistreated by young men because of
her lack of financial security, and Dido is mistreated because
of her race.

The Lord Chief Justice's household is particular about
maintaining the rules of their culture; Dido is not able to eat
with the rest of the family when guests are over. However,
the Lord Chief Justice himself breaks convention on several
occasions, commissioning a portrait of Dido and Elizabeth
that portrays them as equals.

Dido is relieved when he rules against the slave traders.
He also supports her decision to marry a clergyman who
loves her, rather than a gentleman who wants to marry her
for her money and who says he can overlook her mixed race.

The Adoption Connection

Belle is set in England in the late 1700s while the slave trade was still legal and tensions regarding it were brewing. Dido's father placed her with his extended family when she was a young child, and her extended relatives raised her. They initially accepted her because it was their duty, but they were uncomfortable accepting her because of her race.

In time, they came to love her. The Lord Chief Justice comments to his wife that he loves Dido as though she was born to him.

When Dido learns as a young adult that her father has died she expresses regret that she had not met him a second time. Her great-uncle and great-aunt continue to fill parental roles for her.

Elizabeth's father abandoned her in favor of the family he starts with his new wife. Troubled by this loss years later, Elizabeth expresses a belief that all men always leave.

Strong Points

The Lord Chief Justice's love for Dido is often apparent.

Dido asserts that she will not apologize for her lineage.

Dido and Elizabeth have developed a strong sisterly bond.

Challenges

Some of the racist attitudes held by those around Dido are hard to stomach.

A man is somewhat violent towards Dido.

Recommendations

Belle is a beautiful, thought-provoking film. It captures the formation of what is essentially an adoptive family and shows the love that grows between Dido and her great-uncle.

This film seems best suited to adults, who might enjoy its slow pace and profound story.

Questions for Discussion

- Do you view your child's pre-adoption history and family tree with honor or shame?

- How do you rate the Lord Chief Justice as a parent?

- What do you hope for the relationships your children will have with each other?

Big Daddy

(1999, PG, 93 minutes. Live Action. Starring Adam Sandler, Cole and Dylan Sprouse, Joey Lauren Adams, and Jon Stewart)

The Plot

Sonny Koufax is an underachieving law school graduate. Instead of taking the bar exam, he has chosen to live off the proceeds of a car accident settlement and works one day a week at a toll booth. His girlfriend threatens to leave him if he does not grow up.

When Sonny's roommate Kevin is away on business, a child shows up at Sonny's door. Julian is five years old and has a note from his dying mother that says she cannot care for him anymore. The note says that Kevin is his father. Sonny calls Kevin, who denies having a son.

Sonny decides to use Julian to his advantage, thinking that having a son will make him seem more mature to his girlfriend. Sonny lies to a social worker and says that he is Kevin. Sonny is disappointed to find that his girlfriend has already decided to leave him.

Sonny keeps Julian in an attempt to save Julian from going to a group home, and also uses Julian to break the ice with a new girlfriend.

Sonny also starts to see the importance of structure in parenting and he begins to take responsibility for Julian's social development. However, the social worker discovers that Sonny has lied about his identity.

In court, Sonny tries to convince a judge that he should be allowed to continue parenting Julian. The judge declines, but Sonny is spared jail time when Kevin remembers a drunken night he had that did lead to Julian's birth. Kevin assumes a paternal role for Julian, and Sonny promises to always be Julian's friend and family.

The Adoption Connection

After Julian unexpectedly arrives in Sonny's life, Sonny functions as a foster father to him. Sonny learns the importance of responsible parenting rather quickly, and shifts from seeing Julian as a fun novelty to loving him as a son.

When Julian is forcibly taken away from Sonny by a social worker, Julian protests and Sonny is dejected.

Julian is eventually placed with his birth father, whom he had never met, but maintains a close relationship with Sonny as well.

Strong Points

Big Daddy depicts the growth of a parental relationship between a first-time father and a kindergartener. Sonny initially has a self-centered approach to parenting but develops responsibility and love for Julian. Julian also comes to love and trust Sonny. Foster and adoptive families might find this aspect of the film mirrors their own experiences.

Sonny raises Julian with the help of his friends, showing the benefit of a strong support system.

Even though Sonny and Julian are not able to be father and son, Sonny affirms that his care for Julian will continue forever.

Challenges

Some of the film's humor is crass; Sonny teaches Julian to urinate on restaurants that do not let him use their bathrooms.

The social worker assigned to Julian's case initially ignores signals that should have raised concern—Sonny expressed his desire to put Julian in foster care a couple times. The worker also initially failed to discover that Sonny was impersonating Julian's father.

Sonny's father has a very low opinion of Sonny and berates him for intending to adopt Julian. This might remind some adoptive parents of negative reactions that they received from unsupportive friends or family.

The scene in which Julian is removed from Sonny by the social worker, which features a close-up shot of their hands being pulled apart, could be hard to watch for parents who have experienced a disrupted adoption, parents who have had kids taken from them involuntarily, or children who remember or wonder about being removed from their families of origin.

Julian expresses that he wants Sonny to be his dad. He doesn't get his wish, but his situation does turn out happily.

Recommendations

Big Daddy varies between being crass and silly at times and being heartwarming and emotional at others. It could be an interesting date night movie for parents who are considering adoption or who are early in their adoption journey.

It's particularly interesting for its depiction of a parental relationship developing between a first-time parent and a newly placed child.

Questions for Discussion

- How did your friends and family respond when you told them of your desire to adopt?

- In what ways has your journey towards parenthood gone differently than you expected? Which hard situations have turned out happily? Which might still turn out happily?

- What was your experience of the social workers, lawyers, and judges involved in your journey towards parenthood?

- How do parental relationships form between parents and newborns? How is it different when the parental relationship starts when the child is older? How is it similar?

- What role do you imagine Sonny will continue to have in Julian's life?

The Blind Side

(2009, PG-13, 126 minutes. Live Action. Biopic of Michael Oher,
starring Sandra Bullock, Tim McGraw, and Quinton Aaron)

The Plot

Seventeen-year-old Michael Oher has bounced from sofa
to sofa, and in and out of foster care, since being detained
from his mother when he was seven years old. He has never
known his father but learns that his father has recently died.

Michael is admitted into a private Christian school in
spite of his very low grade point average (GPA), largely
because a coach believes that he will be an asset to the
school's sports program.

While at the school, Michael is noticed by Leann Tuohy,
the mother of another high-school student. Leann realizes
that Michael does not have a place to sleep and invites him
into her home. Over time, this one-night visit grows into a
permanent commitment as the Tuohys and Michael begin to
view each other as family.

The genuineness of the Tuohys' love for Michael is
questioned by a National Collegiate Athletic Association
(NCAA) investigator who wonders whether the Tuohys
took Michael in only to ensure that he played football for
their preferred college. This causes Michael anxiety, but the
Tuohys are able to convince him that their love for him is
unconditional.

Michael does end up playing college football at their
preferred school and is drafted in the first round of the
NFL Draft.

The Adoption Connection

Michael was taken into the Tuohy home as an informal placement. By the end of the film, the Tuohys have asked him whether he would like to join their family through legal guardianship. When Michael is unsure what that means, they explain that it would make him part of their family. He replies that he already feels as though they are a family.

Michael has a brother who he hasn't seen in 10 years.

Strong Points

The Tuohy family fully embraces Michael.

Leann speaks up for Michael when her friends speak unkindly of him and corrects them when they portray her involvement in his life as merely a charitable endeavor.

Michael does benefit from the Tuohys' kindness, but he is also appreciated by them for his own character strengths.

The Tuohys extend their home and family to Michael, but they do ask him whether he wants to stay, and later they ask him whether he wants to be a part of the family. They give him the power to choose and he replies that he doesn't want to leave.

Leann is shocked that the state would allow her to take guardianship of Michael without consulting his mother. Leann finds Michael's mother and speaks to her before assuming guardianship of Michael. Leann tells Mrs. Oher that Mrs. Oher will always be Michael's mother; she offers to arrange a meeting between the two, but Mrs. Oher declines. Leann's intentional efforts to include Mrs. Oher are respectful and positive.

Challenges

Leann does not adopt Michael. She believes that it wouldn't make sense to do so, since he's almost 18. However, adoption forms a legally binding familial relationship that continues throughout adulthood. Right now, any kids Michael has will be "like grandkids" to the Tuohys; if they adopt him, any kids he has will legally be their grandkids.

Leann's husband seems to go along with Leann's desire to make Michael a part of their family, but his own feelings aren't fully explored.

An unexpected car accident could be jarring to viewers who have experienced similar accidents or other violence.

Michael revisits some of his childhood peers, but the situation quickly turns dangerous.

For Michael's graduation, Leann provides a baby picture to be projected on a screen so that Michael's walk across the stage is similar to his classmates, but she confides to someone that the picture is from an advertisement.

Recommendations

The Blind Side can be helpful for people who are considering foster care. It can help prospective foster and adoptive parents develop empathy for the experiences that kids in foster care may have had, while also encouraging those parents to remember to look deeper than initial reports about a kid. This is a good choice for a parents' movie night.

Questions for Discussion

- Michael is described as a person who runs away, who also struggles academically. What elements of his life circumstance feed into that? How has Michael compared to the expectations that people likely had of him after reading his file?

- What did legal guardianship accomplish for Michael that long-term foster care could not have accomplished? What could adoption have accomplished that legal guardianship could not have accomplished?

- How do you want to affect the lives of the children who you bring into your home, whether through birth, foster care, or adoption?

Camp

(2013, PG-13, 109 minutes. Live Action. Starring Miles Elliot, Michael Mattera, and Grace Johnson)

The Plot

Ten-year-old Eli is neglected by his mother, but he is only removed from her home when his alcoholic father attacks him. His mother dies of a drug overdose shortly afterwards.

Eli is placed in a group home and gains a reputation there for biting other children.

Eli is able to attend a Christian camp for foster children where he is assigned Ken as a personal counselor. Ken is a young executive who has only volunteered at the camp to impress a wealthy potential client.

Ken begins caring about Eli when he learns Eli's story but his self-centeredness surfaces frequently as he is frustrated by Eli's hard-to-control behaviors. Eventually, Ken has a change of heart that allows him to care unselfishly about Eli.

Eventually, Eli's incarcerated father asks Ken to take placement of Eli.

The Adoption Connection

The film *Camp* is based on a real-life camp that hosts foster kids for a week of fun.

Eli's journey into foster care is not uncommon; he was neglected by one parent and abused by another. In the group home, his behaviors have gained him a negative reputation.

Eli seems to be short on options after his mother dies of a drug overdose and his dad is incarcerated, but his counselor from camp takes placement of him. Placement with "non-related extended family members" is a desirable option for kids in foster care; non-related extended family members can be family friends, coaches, teachers, or almost any other adult who has a pre-existing relationship with the child. *Camp* captures one way that placements like that can be made.

Two sisters see each other at the camp; this is the only time they will see each other all year.

Strong Points

The film captures the love that volunteers are able to share with kids in foster care and the kids' response to a week filled with kindness and affirmation.

The film shows how relationships can develop between kids and their caregivers over time.

An experienced counselor wisely understands that children cannot be held accountable to know good behavior if it has not been modeled for them. His approach seems to be one of patience and redirection rather than punishment and shame, which seems more likely to work well with most children and perhaps especially foster children.

A camp director tells Ken that it is unrealistic to expect a child to heal rapidly from years of pain.

Although it would be easy to vilify Eli's abusive father, we learn that he, too, was abused as a child. Nearly all behaviors make sense within a certain context; it doesn't mean that the behaviors are acceptable, but they do come from somewhere and understanding that can help us see the humanity of a person rather than just viewing them as a caricatured villain. It will be helpful for Eli's future caregivers to find a way to see some value and some redeeming factors in Eli's father.

Challenges

While they are at camp, Ken tells Eli that Eli is bad. Ken's motivation for helping at the camp is initially poor.

The incidents of neglect and abuse that Eli experiences are believable, and they will be hard to watch for some viewers.

In a moment of anger, Eli tells another child that no one will ever come to take him home.

Recommendations

Some scenes of abuse in the early parts of this film and a later scene in which Eli's dad drunkenly enters the camp could make the film scary or sad for many young viewers to watch. If those scenes are omitted, the camp scenes could be enjoyable for kids of ages 8 and up, but the film as a whole seems best geared towards adults and perhaps some mature, older teenagers.

As you watch it, imagine the experiences that your children might have had before coming into your home, and imagine how their experiences might influence their behaviors. Also, consider finding nontraditional ways to help kids in foster care. Are there any camps near you where you could serve?

Questions for Discussion

- How can your family help kids in foster care?

- Did Eli's behaviors reflect Eli's character or did they reflect his experiences and emotions? How can you tell the difference? What difference does the distinction make?

- How do you expect your next children to come into your lives?

- Eli frequently tells Ken that he hates him. Why does Eli say that? What would your response be if a child told you that, if you understood why they said it? What would be the best response for the child to receive?

- What behavioral expectations do you have of the children who will be placed with you? Are they likely to be immediately realistic for those kids?

- Eli's father is worried that Eli will follow in his footsteps. What might make that less likely? What can help Eli thrive?

Delivery Man

(2013, PG-13, 105 minutes. Live Action. Starring
Vince Vaughn, Chris Pratt, and Cobie Smulders)

The Plot

David Wozniak works at his family's meat market but he has always been a bit strapped for cash. As a college student, he donated sperm to a sperm bank several hundred times in exchange for $25,000. He was told that his identity would remain confidential.

A couple of decades have passed. Now his girlfriend is pregnant with what he believes will be his first child and he is being pursued by thugs to whom he owes $80,000. At the same time, he learns that the sperm bank made a mistake and provided his sperm to all of their clients; he has 533 biological children and 142 of them have filed a lawsuit to learn his identity.

David covertly gets to know many of his children and wants to reveal himself to them. However, his lawyer advises him that if he keeps his identity a secret and sues the clinic, he will make enough money to pay off his pursuers.

David initially follows his lawyer's advice, but when he tells his father his situation his father pays off his debts. With his debts repaid, David is able to reveal himself to the 142 young adults who want to know him.

In the last few moments of the film, David's girlfriend gives birth to his 534th child. While visiting her in the hospital, David proposes to her and also tells her about his 533 other children. She is initially upset at the revelation and tells him that he is no longer the father of the newborn baby. However, he asserts that she cannot take away his fatherhood and says that his decision to care for his hundreds of kids should convince her that he will be a good dad.

She quickly decides to stay with David, and begins to show the new baby to the dozens and dozens of his half-siblings who have come to the hospital to celebrate.

The Adoption Connection

The question of guaranteed confidentiality is often included in discussions about opening adoption records. Through anonymous sperm donations, David has become the unknown and unknowing father to hundreds. When his children want to discover his identity, a court must decide whether David's guaranteed right to confidentiality legally trumps the perceived need of his children to find him.

The court agrees that David's right to confidentiality must be honored, but David's children remind him through a news interview that, while the court case allows him to remain confidential, it does not require him to do so.

David eventually chooses to establish a relationship with his children even though he is not required to. Eventually, David asserts his right to be the father of his children, both the one born to his girlfriend and the many that he did not know.

Strong Points

Before they learn David's identity, his children are reminded that, even though they are still looking for their father, they have found each other.

David's own sense of what is right eventually trumps the confidentiality to which he is legally entitled.

David's children are all unique, and each child who hopes to know him has a highly individualized reason for wanting that relationship.

The film makes a point that might help some adults empathize with adopted people who want an open relationship with their birth family—the child is the one most affected by the confidentiality, but the only one who did not willingly agree to be bound by it.

Challenges

When David says that his girlfriend, siblings, and father are the ones who are really his family, he deeply hurts the feelings of his adult son Vigo. Vigo reminds him that, although

David has moved on from his past, the children he created are real and are also his family. The scene demonstrates the importance of language and word choice in relationships touched by adoption, including reunification.

Recommendations

Delivery Man is a surprisingly fun film for parents, although the subject matter probably limits it to an adult audience. *Delivery Man* could be a good choice for adoptive parents and people considering adoption, as it can encourage them to consider the need their children may feel to know their birth parents.

Questions for Discussion

- Should confidentiality in matters of adoption be legislated or left to individual consciences?

- Why did David's children want to know him?

- Should the court have sided with David or with his children?

- How would you feel if a child you adopted wanted to know about their birth parents?

- How would you feel if a child you adopted wanted to actually know their birth parents?

- What is the effect of using terms like "real family"? Why do people use those terms? Are they meant to include certain people or to exclude certain people? Which terms might be better?

- David says that only the father can decide whether he is the father. What does he mean by that? Do you agree?

I Am Sam

(2001, PG-13, 134 minutes. Live Action. Starring Sean Penn, Michelle Pfeiffer, Dianne Wiest, and Dakota Fanning)

The Plot

Sam Dawson's daughter, Lucy, is the driving motivation of his life. He has a developmental disability, and he and Lucy were abandoned by Lucy's mother outside of the hospital just after Lucy was born.

With the help of some friends, Sam has raised Lucy for the first few years of her life. Now as a young grade-school student, Lucy is uncomfortable with the thought that she might be more intellectually advanced than her father, who has been evaluated as having the intellectual level of a seven-year-old.

When Sam is arrested due to a misunderstanding, Lucy is taken into foster care. Her foster parents are gracious with Sam and support visits, but they also want to adopt Lucy.

Although Sam begins to believe that he cannot take care of Lucy, her foster parents see his devoted love for Lucy and his desire to meet her needs. Touched, her foster mother changes her mind, and suggests that she will tell the court that Sam can be Lucy's parent.

Sam is joyfully reunited with Lucy, and he now has a much broader support system that includes Lucy's former foster parents.

The Adoption Connection

Lucy spends some time in foster care. During the course of her time in care, her strong desire to be with Sam is evident; she tricks him into running away with her, and at other times she runs away from her foster home to be with him. When Sam fails to come to some of his parental visits, Lucy becomes enraged at him. Even while in foster care, Lucy looks to Sam for validation and approval.

Lucy tells Sam some horror stories she hears from other children in placement: one has had five different mothers and one was hit by a foster parent.

Lucy has told a classmate that she is adopted; it is untrue, but she says it because she is embarrassed by her classmates' teasing about her father's intellectual challenges.

Strong Points

Sam's love for his daughter is very evident throughout the film. The film shows that, although he cannot do it alone, he is able to meet Lucy's needs with the help of a robust support system.

The film depicts Lucy's love for her father and her strong longing to be with him.

Lucy's foster mother finds it bittersweet to recommend reunification but does it anyway, believing it is the right outcome. She confides in Sam that she always wanted to be a mother; he affirms that she has a very important place in Lucy's life and heart.

After Sam and Lucy reunify, Lucy's foster parents remain involved in her life. That's an ideal outcome for foster care: reunification into a healthier family of origin, perpetually supported by the people who have come to love the child while she was in foster care.

Challenges

In what could be a misleading scene, it seems as though Lucy's foster mother makes the decision that allows Sam to reunify with Lucy. In real life, foster parents often feel frustratingly powerless; although foster parents can give their perspective, decisions about a child's permanency are typically made by social workers and judges.

We know only very little about Lucy's mother.

Sometimes Lucy seems to take a parental role over Sam.

Recommendations

The primary goal of foster care is reunification; adoption is a secondary goal. Sam's challenges, Lucy's behaviors, Sam's failure to come to some visits, and the incident in which Sam and Lucy appeared to run away together would be fuel for some arguments against reunification; *I Am Sam* makes a case as to why reunification is still worth pursuing.

I Am Sam can introduce a helpful perspective of a birth parent in the foster care system as someone who loves their child but has a hard time meeting their child's needs. It highlights Sam's emotional pain when a judge orders Lucy to be detained and the sadness for Sam and Lucy when a social worker pries them apart from each other. It also shows how deeply Lucy loves Sam. *I Am Sam* can help prospective foster parents develop empathy for the birth parents of their future foster children—and for the children.

Parents who are hoping to adopt from foster care sometimes find it difficult to root for reunification; it seems to be at cross purposes with their strong desires to grow their family and to ensure that the children they've come to care about are truly safe.

I Am Sam seems like an excellent choice for foster parents and for adults considering becoming foster parents—especially for those who are hoping for foster care to be an avenue towards adoption.

Questions for Discussion

- What were the strongest reasons for Lucy to be adopted by her foster parents? What were the strongest reasons for her to reunify with Sam? Which reasons do you find more compelling? Imagine answering this last question as if you were Lucy's foster parents; then as Sam; then as Lucy; then as a judge or social worker.

- What services will help Sam continue to care for Lucy?

- How involved in Lucy's life do you believe her foster parents will be, now that she has reunified with Sam? How big of a difference will they make in her life? How hard will it be for them? Do you think they will say it's worth it?

- If the foster parents had adopted Lucy, do you believe they would have allowed an ongoing relationship between Lucy and Sam? What reservations would they have about that relationship? What benefits would result from that relationship? Which list of reasons is most compelling?

- What preconceptions do you have about parents whose children are in foster care? How does this movie challenge the universality of those preconceptions?

- Is it reasonable to expect foster children to stop loving their birth parents once they are adopted?

Ida

(2013, PG-13, 82 minutes. Live Action. Black and
White; in Polish with English subtitles. Starring Agata
Trzebuchowska, Agata Kulesza, and Dawid Ogrodnik)
Award: 2015 Adoption at the Movies Special
Award for Best Foreign Film

The Plot

In a post-World-War-II Polish convent, Anna is preparing to make her vows to join the convent for life. Before she will be allowed to join, she is required to find her aunt, Wanda Gruz, who is her only living relative.

Anna learns much from Wanda: Anna's birth name is Ida Lebenstein; she was raised by the nuns after being taken to the convent as an infant. Anna's parents were Jews who died during the Nazi occupation of Poland. Wanda had served as a Communist judge, condemning people to death.

Anna wishes to find her parents' graves; her search leads her to the home of Feliks, who eventually confesses that he killed them. Shortly after this, Wanda commits suicide. Anna explores her aunt's lifestyle of drinking, smoking, and sex, but ultimately returns to the convent.

The Adoption Connection

Anna has been raised by nuns and never knew her parents. Although Anna protests, her convent requires her to seek information about her birth family before taking her lifetime vows.

What she learns about her family is painful; her aunt lives a lifestyle that Anna considers immoral, and her parents were murdered. However, learning about her past appears to help Anna as she makes major decisions about her life. In meeting her aunt, Anna learns her heritage, her family's history, the city she was born in, and her birth name.

Strong Points

Anna is encouraged by her convent to learn about her past before making decisions that will direct her future. It appears that the journey is helpful to her.

Challenges

Some of what Anna learns is very sad, but Anna is still able to learn it, process it, and move on into adulthood. However, Anna's aunt does not find a way to process what she learns, and ultimately jumps to her death from a high window.

Recommendations

Like the excellent documentary *Closure*, *Ida* is about a woman entering her young adulthood and trying to find out about her birth family. In *Ida*, the search is fictional and post-Holocaust, and occurs after her parents have died.

It is a sad but beautiful and thoughtful award-winning film that seems most likely to appeal to adults.

As you watch it, consider how Anna is affected—and even helped—by learning her history, even though it is traumatic.

Questions for Discussion

- What is one of the hardest things you've ever been able to forgive?

- The history that Anna learns is particularly heartbreaking, but it seems to help her. For the children that you adopt, how can you help them learn and process the difficult parts of their histories, in an age-appropriate way? What benefits might they gain from knowing even the harder parts of their stories? How can you phrase the hard parts of your child's story in honest but age-appropriate ways?

- If there are some aspects of your child's story that you do not think should be disclosed to your child right now, when should they learn them, and how? (If there are some parts of their story that are exceptionally traumatic, it would be wise to consult with an adoption-specialized therapist to figure out how to proceed.)

Martian Child

(2007, PG, 106 minutes. Live Action. Starring
John Cusack and Bobby Coleman)

The Plot

Science fiction author David Gordon and his wife Mary became certified to adopt a child but Mary passed away before they were matched with a child.

Two years after her death, David receives a call from a social worker saying that the agency has a child who might be a good match with David.

Dennis is a young boy who says that he believes he is from Mars. Over time, and with the help of David's friends, family, and aging dog, David and Dennis each grow past their insecurities and learn to become a family.

The Adoption Connection

Dennis appears to have been living at a group home prior to coming to live with David.

Dennis was abandoned by a previous set of parents. He cannot understand why that happened, and his claim of being from Mars seems to be his way of coping with his sense of rejection and his fear that he will not be able to stay in a family.

David has some doubt about whether he can be a successful single parent to a child with the needs that Dennis presents, but eventually he and Dennis have a dramatic, heartfelt conversation that cements their status as a family.

David and Mary initially decided to pursue adoption because Mary was an adoptee.

Strong Points

David has an honest insecurity about whether he will succeed as an adoptive parent; a close friend assures him that his willingness to evaluate himself honestly rather than rushing in overconfidently is an indication that he will likely be a good adoptive parent.

David articulates how important and sensible it is for him to provide loving stability to Dennis.

David is willing to be unorthodox in order to connect with Dennis and help Dennis feel comfortable. Dennis says that he will only eat Lucky Charms, so David fills a shopping cart with the sugary cereal. He encourages Dennis to break plates so that he can prove to Dennis that he cares about Dennis more than he cares about his belongings.

David is imperfect and sometimes insecure but he loves Dennis, and his love is effective. He also directly addresses Dennis' past abandonment, saying that he will never abandon Dennis and that those who abandoned him made a huge mistake. This appears to be monumental in Dennis' healing.

Challenges

David's sister expresses some pessimistic and stereotypical thoughts about Dennis in particular and adopted kids in general. David generally responds well to her discouragement.

A social worker on Dennis' case seem quick to judge David's approach to parenting and almost pulls Dennis out of David's home.

After they have been through many ordeals, David tells Dennis that he might not be a good parent for Dennis. Dennis runs away, fearing abandonment. David has to track Dennis down and convince Dennis that he will not abandon him.

Recommendations

Martian Child seems best suited to adults who have adopted or who are considering adoption.

David deals with his sister's cautions and his own doubts about his ability to be a single parent, which could make this film helpful for other single adoptive parents. Because the film offers a rare portrayal of a single man pursuing adoption, it could be especially significant for single adoptive dads.

Dennis' most foundational unmet need was a sense of permanency in a family. Without that, he could not fully trust or love David; once he had it, he ran to David with a heartfelt embrace.

After watching this movie, think about how Maslow's (1943) Hierarchy of Needs (see Chapter 1) applies to your child and about how you have met and can continue to meet their deepest needs.

Questions for Discussion

- What types of reactions did you receive from your family and friends when you decided to adopt? How did you deal (internally and externally) with any negative or unsupportive things that were said?

- Do you (or did you) have any insecurities about your ability to function as an adoptive parent?

- What reasons led you to adopt?

- People unfamiliar with Dennis' mindset might believe that he is a thief, because he takes things that do not belong to him. How did David understand what Dennis was doing? Which of your kids' behaviors make sense within a certain context, even if they are difficult for others to understand?

- Which of David's emotions interplayed with his pursuit of adoption? How did Dennis' emotions affect his adjustment to David's care?

Moonrise Kingdom

(2012, PG-13, 94 minutes. Live Action. Starring
Bruce Willis, Edward Norton, Bill Murray, Jared
Gilman, Kara Hayward, and Tilda Swinton)

The Plot

It's the mid-1960s. Twelve-year-olds Sam and Suzy met a year ago at a church play and have been pen pals ever since. Suzy is the unhappy daughter of two unhappy lawyers; Sam is a foster child on the verge of being removed from his foster home. He is on a Khaki Scout camping trip, but is treated poorly by the other boys.

Through their letters, Sam and Suzy arrange to run away together; they meet in a field and take off for a secluded cove, where they kiss, dance, and sleep next to each other. They are eventually found by a search party consisting of the Scouts, Suzy's parents, and a police captain.

Suzy is returned to her parents but Social Services is called for Sam, since his foster parents refuse to take him back home. Social Services suggests that Sam will be placed in a group home and given electroshock therapy.

Sam tries to escape by climbing to the top of a tall building during a storm, but the police captain talks Sam down and decides to become Sam's legal guardian. Sam seems to fit well with him; in the last scene of the film, Sam visits Suzy while dressed in a junior-sized police uniform.

The Adoption Connection

Sam is a foster child. He seems to keep to himself but eagerly accepts Captain Sharp's offer to live with him. He appears to thrive once he gets a permanent home.

Sam's experience of being unexpectedly moved from a foster home, and his fear of Social Services, might be familiar to some viewers who have been through foster care.

Suzy tells Sam that she wishes she was an orphan; Sam tells her that she is talking nonsense.

Strong Points

Sam is brave, resourceful, and sometimes insightful; he reminds Suzy that her parents still love her, even when she feels as if they don't.

Challenges

It's frustrating to see Sam's foster father rather emotionlessly report that he cannot accept Sam back into his home; as a reason, he says simply that Sam is emotionally disturbed.

A scene between Sam and Suzy might be uncomfortable or awkward for some viewers; Suzy and Sam get partially undressed and dance together, and Suzy awkwardly invites Sam to touch her chest.

Recommendations

Moonrise Kingdom and *Martian Child* both feature a single man making a parental commitment to a preteen boy on the ledge of a tall building; the characters seem more fully developed in *Martian Child*. However, *Moonrise Kingdom* is a unique, quirky, preteen love story that gives a well-rounded introduction to a 12-year-old boy whom the child welfare system has labeled "disturbed."

Moonrise Kingdom could be a fun film for a parents' movie night. After watching it, talk about the importance of permanency for kids, and remember what it was like to be a preteen.

Questions for Discussion

- In your experience, how do the social workers and the Social Service system that you've worked with compare to *Moonrise Kingdom*'s Social Services?

- What do you think life is like from each of your kids' points of view?

- How much consideration should parents give to labels that the Social Service system places on kids? What is the proper function of those labels?

- What impact did Captain Sharp make on Sam? How did it happen?

- If you have adopted from foster care, compare the way your home felt before adoptive placement with the way it felt after adoptive placement.

ReMoved

(2013, Not rated, 13 minutes. Live Action.
Starring Abby White and Kyra Locke)
Award: 2015 Adoption at the Movies Award for Best Short Film

The Plot

In this short film, grade-school-age Zoe is removed from her parents' home after an incident of domestic violence. Although she tries to run away, she is taken to a foster home. Her infant brother is taken to another home.

Her first foster home is abusive, so she is brought to a second home. Her new foster mother is Kyra, a single teacher. Zoe's behaviors perplex Kyra, but Kyra does not have Zoe removed.

Zoe sees Kyra on the phone and believes that Kyra is calling a social worker to have Zoe taken away, but Zoe is overjoyed when she sees instead that the call results in a social worker bringing her infant brother to her home.

The Adoption Connection

ReMoved mirrors the story of many children in foster care. Zoe's behaviors might be difficult for some foster parents to understand, but the film shows that her behaviors make sense in the context of Zoe's experiences. An understanding, dedicated foster parent is able to provide Zoe with stability, safety, and even a connection with her infant brother.

Many children are adopted from foster care each year; *ReMoved* depicts what the first experiences of that journey might be like.

Strong Points

This film was made by a couple who were inspired by a video they saw during the trainings they attended as part of the process of becoming foster parents. It is insightful and powerful and it has reached millions of viewers with a piercing look at foster care from a child's perspective.

The film is both realistic and hopeful in its portrayal of Zoe, her behaviors, her monitored visits with her mother, her deep care for her brother, and the course of her case.

The film affirms that a child's past trauma is not the child's fault and does not have to determine the child's future.

Challenges

ReMoved is deeply emotional and could be quite triggering to young viewers who have experienced similar losses and similar abuse.

Recommendations

ReMoved is very powerful. Although it is about a child and told from the child's perspective, it seems best reserved for adults and perhaps some older teens who have processed their pasts. It could be helpful for prospective foster parents and their teenage and preteen children, as it can help them understand the possible experiences of their potential future family members.

As you watch it, allow yourself to develop a sense of empathy and understanding for what your children or future children have experienced and reflect on how important it is for Zoe to have a safe, un-abusive home that does not give up on her. The film and its sequel can be accessed at: www.removedfilm.com/pages/watch.

Questions for Discussion

- When Zoe yells at Kyra that she hates her, what is driving that behavior? What do you think of Kyra's response?

- What does Zoe need most?

- What expectations do you have of children in foster care? Is it important to respond to their behaviors in the same way that you would respond to those behaviors from other children? Is it fair to take their histories into account when responding to their behaviors?

- How important is it that siblings be placed together?

Remember My Story: ReMoved Part 2

(2015, Not rated, 23 minutes. Live Action. Starring
Abby White, Kyra Locke, and Benaiah Matanick)

The Plot

In the sequel to *ReMoved*, Zoe is living at her foster home with Kyra and they have taken placement of Zoe's toddler brother, Benaiah. However, Benaiah is placed with a prospective adoptive family while Zoe is left with Kyra.

In a visit with Zoe, Zoe's mother says that she will try to regain custody of Benaiah, but not of Zoe, since Zoe is older. Out of her pain, Zoe acts explosively towards Kyra. The professionals on the case want to respond to Zoe's behavior by medicating Zoe, but Kyra understands the emotional causes of Zoe's behavior and voices her concern that medication isn't what Zoe needs. Kyra also provides Zoe with a way of conceptualizing her tumultuous life experiences, which is helpful to Zoe.

Zoe is not able to return to her mother, but it does appear that she is able to see Benaiah throughout her childhood.

In a closing scene, a grown-up Zoe has become a teacher and she demonstrates empathy and understanding for a young child in her class who is finding it difficult to be in foster care.

The Adoption Connection

It's not clear whether Zoe was adopted. She was not able to reunify with her birth mother, but did remain in contact with her brother throughout her childhood.

She ultimately followed in the footsteps of her foster mother to become a teacher. As a teacher, Zoe incorporates her own childhood experiences to help other children.

Remember My Story: ReMoved Part 2 completes the story of the first *ReMoved* film, and together they provide an insightful look into many aspects of a child's journey through foster care.

Strong Points

Kyra acts non-defensively when Zoe yells at her. Kyra is consistently understanding, and Zoe benefits from that both immediately and into her adulthood.

Like its predecessor, this film is realistic and hopeful about Zoe, her journey through foster care, and her transition into adulthood. The film is gripping, and can encourage prospective foster and adoptive parents to have empathy and understanding for the children they will parent.

Challenges

It seems as though Zoe and Benaiah do not get to live together; they see each other, but in real life it would have almost certainly been better for them to stay together. It is heartbreaking to watch Zoe discover that her brother is no longer going to live with her.

Recommendations

Like *ReMoved*, this film can be seen online at www. removedfilm.com/pages/watch. Zoe's story is sad and painful but also hopeful and ultimately uplifting.

This film is best geared towards adults, and possibly teenagers. As you watch it, consider the importance of permanency for kids in foster care. Think about how you can ensure that a child in your care has a permanent place to call home, and reflect on the importance of sibling relationships. Spend some time considering who your child may become and how their past can form them into a person of strength, compassion, and wisdom.

Questions for Discussion

- Zoe recovered from Benaiah's move into another home, but what would have been the benefit of him staying in placement with her?

- Why did the professionals want to put Zoe on medication? Why did Zoe's foster mother disagree? Do you think Zoe needed medicine or something else?

- How do you view Zoe's birth mother?

- Zoe storms into Kyra's classroom and yells at her, saying that what has happened is Kyra's fault. Where is Zoe's anger coming from? How would the situation have turned out differently if Kyra had become offended or defensive? How do you imagine you would react if a child did the same thing towards you? What would be the best possible reaction? How can you prepare ahead of time to make it more likely that your reaction in the heat of the moment will be the best possible reaction?

- Zoe is likely sad whenever each of her visits with Benaiah ends; even though she will be sad at the end, do you feel the visits are important?

- How did the grown-up Zoe use her childhood experiences to help others? What impact did Kyra make on Zoe's life?

St. Vincent

(2014, PG-13, 102 minutes. Live Action. Starring Bill Murray,
Melissa McCarthy, Jaeden Lieberher, and Naomi Watts)

The Plot

When Maggie Bronstein and her 12-year-old son, Oliver,
move in next door to Vincent MacKenna, their moving van
causes damage to his car and a tree in his front yard. Vincent
is a cranky old man; he demands payment for the damage
and shows no other interest in Maggie or Oliver.

After his first day of school, Oliver is locked out of his
home and Maggie will not be able to come home until her
work shift ends. Oliver stays with Vincent. Vincent charges
Maggie for babysitting but offers to continue watching
Oliver each afternoon so long as Maggie pays him.

Vincent is in debt, and he has been investing much of his
money into a top-quality nursing home for his wife, Sandy,
who suffers from Alzheimer's disease. Vincent has become
a frequent patron of the horse races in an attempt to raise
money to keep Sandy in the home, but unlucky bets have
kept him in deep debt to dangerous people.

Maggie's estranged husband learns that Vincent has
taken Oliver to some unsavory places while babysitting and
uses this information to get joint custody of Oliver.

Maggie forbids Oliver to see Vincent, but Oliver has
come to care about Vincent. He uncovers Vincent's history,
and learns that Vincent has been a war hero and a devoted
husband.

Oliver's school presents a program in which students are
asked to name a modern-day saint and Oliver nominates
Vincent. His presentation touches Vincent's heart and also

changes his parents' minds; Oliver and Vincent are able to continue spending time together, and it seems that Vincent will be accepted as part of Oliver's extended family.

The Adoption Connection

Maggie confides to a school administrator that she and her estranged husband adopted Oliver. Maggie has been hurt by her husband's infidelity and comments to the administrator that she believes her infertility was caused by her body rejecting her husband's sperm.

Oliver confides in a friend that he misses his dad. Oliver's mom left his dad because of his dad's affairs. Vincent serves as something of a father figure to Oliver; he's not perfect, but he does teach Oliver how to stand up for himself.

Strong Points

Oliver's compassionate view of Vincent enables him to see the truly good characteristics that lie hidden underneath Vincent's gruff exterior. The film captures the encouraging perspective that there is more to a person than the façade they initially present.

Challenges

Vincent puts Oliver in some unsavory situations; he introduces him to a prostitute, takes him to a bar, and teaches him how to gamble.

One character mentions St. William of Rochester, the patron saint of adopted children, but notes that he was killed by the boy he adopted.

Oliver has frequently overheard his mother speaking ill of his father; she is surprised to learn that he has heard and remembered all that she has said.

Recommendations

St. Vincent is an interesting study of the relationship between a 12-year-old boy and his curmudgeonly neighbor. Oliver's adoption is incidental to the story. The heart of the film lies in Oliver's ability to see Vincent with wise, compassionate eyes. The development of his relationship with Vincent drives the film.

St. Vincent would be an interesting choice for an adult movie night. After watching it, reflect about first impressions, people who have influenced you for good, and the impact you want to have on others, including the kids you love.

Questions for Discussion

• What impact do you want to make on the world?

• Who are some "saints" who have influenced your life in a positive way?

• Who are some people who exceeded your initial impression of them?

• What first impressions did you have upon meeting your children?

• What first impressions do you believe you make on others? How can you know? What do you want those first impressions to be?

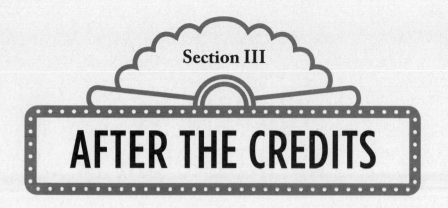

Section III

AFTER THE CREDITS

Movies can be fun and helpful tools as you talk as a family about important adoption issues. However, sometimes families need some outside help to be able to have open, robust, and non-defensive conversations. Even families who are skilled at conversation sometimes need extra guidance to help a family member process deeply traumatic events effectively. In this section, we'll look briefly at what to do when movies aren't enough, and I'll introduce resources that can help families through difficult issues.

Chapter 9

WHEN MOVIES AREN'T ENOUGH

Communication is one of the most important parts of family life. Many problems can be traced to breakdowns in communication. Healthy and effective communication can resolve many issues. Communication is what helps us convey love, family values, belongingness, and culture. Communication helps us grow. *Adoption at the Movies* is a tool to help families achieve and model more robust, unguarded, and productive communication, and I believe that, most of the time, it can be a part of helping families grow and thrive.

Communication is like duct tape; it can do almost everything. However, duct tape can't redirect a train speeding off course; that task calls for Superman. The films and discussions introduced in this book can help families move from Secrecy into Confidentiality and from Silence into Well-Timed Conversation. However, family movie nights might not be the only tool you'll need. It could take professional family therapy to introduce stability to an unstable situation, to develop a plan for safety in a physically or emotionally unsafe situation, or to teach families how to have healthy conversations. Once a family is safe, stable, and able to talk, movie nights become a very valuable tool.

In the first chapter, we talked about Maslow's (1943) Hierarchy of Needs and how kids need to feel safe and stable before they can move on to higher-level needs. Movie nights are part of the work of achieving the high level needs of love, belonging, esteem, self-esteem, and self-actualization. If your child's more foundational needs of safety and stability aren't met, it would be most effective first to work towards meeting those needs. If that's the case, therapy may be a good initial step. Consider calling local adoption and foster care offices, or using Psychology Today's Therapist Finder (https://therapists.psychologytoday.com/rms) or a similar website for your local area to find a therapist who specializes in adoption issues.

It's also possible that your child's story has very specific elements that don't appear in any films. You could find films that touch on similar issues or films that focus on the emotions that are part of your child's story, but again it might be helpful to seek professional help to create ways to help your child access their story. Even if it is difficult to figure out how to share your child's story, your child deserves to know the truth in an age-appropriate way. An adoption professional or an adoption-aware therapist can help you prepare to share your child's story in a way that will be helpful rather than harmful.

It's important to remember that although your child's life and your family's story are always touched by adoption, adoption is not the cause of every challenge that you face. Teenagers choosing the esteem of their friends over obedience to their parents sounds a lot like a person with their needs for Love and Belonging already met reaching to meet their needs for Esteem and Self-Esteem. It might be unpleasant—and it might even be wrapped in adoption language—but it is a normal part of development for any teen.

Other challenges such as conflicts with friends at school, academic struggles, dealing with bullies, or dealing with nightmares show up in the lives of people who are adopted and also in the lives of people who are not adopted. Adoption always has the potential to be a factor, but it isn't always actually one.

There is no shame in asking for help—and there is also no shame in asking for help to decide whether you need to ask for help! With good therapeutic help, your family can achieve—or regain—a healthy spot from which to benefit from the discussions that this book introduces.

Chapter 10

WHERE TO GO FROM HERE
ADDITIONAL RESOURCES

With this book and good access to films through Netflix, Amazon, your local library, or (in the US) Redbox, you can have as many conversations as there are movies. Of course, it is always prudent to research a movie before sharing it with your kids.

The *Adoption at the Movies* website (www.adoptionat themovies.com) was created to help families use film to enter into conversations, and it also explores and analyzes the ways that different films present adoption and adoption-related issues, which helps parents decide which movies to watch and which movies to skip. You can check the website for reviews of new, upcoming, and classic films. The site is updated approximately once a week.

You can also check the Adoption Movie Review online database (www.adoptionlcsw.com/p/res.html) to browse through the hundreds of films catalogued and reviewed for adoptive families. While you're at the site, you can subscribe to the free email newsletter so that every new review is delivered straight to you.

Books, like movies, can be useful conversation starters for kids. The four kids' books on adoption that I most recommend are *A Mother for Choco* by Keiko Kasza (1996, first published 1992), *How I Was Adopted* by Joanna Cole (1999, first published 1995), *A Forever Family* by Roslyn Banish with Jennifer Jordan-Wong (1992), and *We Belong Together* by Todd Parr (2007). *A Mother for Choco* does a wonderful job of showing that members of a family do not have to look alike. *How I Was Adopted* is a fictional journey from conception to adoption. *A Forever Family* is a true story told in the words of its 8-year-old subject, and the book's black and white photos accompany Jennifer's memories of travelling through foster care en route to her adoptive family. *We Belong Together* is a bright, bold, colorful book that tells preschoolers who have been adopted that they belong where they are. If you're interested in more kids' books, check out the reviews on the kids' book page of the *Adoption at the Movies* website.

For some parental reading, *The Open-Hearted Way to Open Adoption* (Holden and Hass, 2013) presents a helpful framework for thinking about openness in adoption. It's an excellent read for adoptive parents as well as people considering adopting. Lori Holden, the author, regularly writes about openness in adoption on her site (http://lavenderluz.com).

Three magazines that focus on adoption (and that sometimes cover films from an adoption point of view) are *Adoptive Families* (https://www.adoptivefamilies.com), *Adoption Today* (www.adoptiontoday.com), and *Focus on Adoption* (a Canadian magazine: https://www.bcadoption.com/focus-adoption-magazine).

For background, you might enjoy reading Abraham Maslow's (1943) article on the Hierarchy of Needs.

Silverstein and Kaplan's work on the core issues of adoption (no date, but drawing from their work originally published in 1982) is foundational reading for any person touched by adoption.

The Psychology Today Therapist Finder (https://therapists.psychologytoday.com/rms) is a helpful and user-friendly tool to find therapists in the United States and Canada, sorted by their specialties, locations, fees, and accepted insurances. This is a great tool for finding an adoption-focused therapist in your area.

The Counselling Directory (www.counselling-directory.org.uk/adv-search.html) serves families in the UK and offers an advanced search option that allows users to type in a keyword; typing in "adoption" will bring up any therapists that mention it as a specialty.

Good Therapy Australia (https://www.goodtherapy.com.au) has an advanced search option; users can select "adoption/foster care" as an "area of concern" in order to find therapists who focus on adoption and foster care.

You can find support groups in your area through the North American Council on Adoptable Children's database (serves the US and Canada: www.nacac.org/parentgroups/database.html). You can also find helpful resources for post-adoption parenting through AdoptUSKids (www.adoptuskids.org/for-families/post-adoption-resources).

And of course, stay in touch with Adoption at the Movies on social media (www.facebook.com/adoptionatthemovies and www.twitter.com/adoptionmovies) to find out about adoption themes in movies that you can still catch in the theaters.

Thanks for reading this book! Now let's go watch a movie!

APPENDICES

MOVIES ALPHABETICALLY

MOVIES BY AGE

To help you get started with a movie tonight, here are some suggestions sorted by broad age group. Check out the full reviews in this book to get more precise age recommendations and for some help in figuring out which film best suits your needs. Some movies fit for more than one age group; for example, some of the films listed under "Grown-Ups" only show up there and are movies best suited to parents rather than kids; but other movies listed under "Grown-Ups" are kid-friendly movies that can also hold their own as entertaining and worthwhile for adults, whether or not kids are also in the audience.

Age 7 and Under

- Choose Your Own Adventure: The Abominable Snowman p.**115**
- Curly Top p.**118**
- Despicable Me 2 p.**124**
- Ernest and Celestine p.**129**
- Frozen p.**68**
- Kung Fu Panda p.**135**
- Kung Fu Panda 3 p.**141**
- Penguins of Madagascar p.**153**
- Planes p.**88**
- Planes: Fire and Rescue p.**90**

Ages 7–12

Ages 12–18

Grown-Ups

MOVIES BY
DISCUSSION TOPIC

This non-exhaustive index is to help you find a film to talk about a specific topic. Please check out the full reviews in this book to help you decide which film best suits your needs.

Feeling Abandoned

Absent Parents

Abuse Experienced

- Antwone Fisher p.**214**
- Camp (2013 version) p.**226**
- Cinderella (2015 version) p.**60**
- ReMoved p.**246**
- Secondhand Lions p.**179**

Adoptive Family as Normal Life

- Choose Your Own Adventure: The Abominable Snowman p.**115**
- Despicable Me 2 p.**124**
- Kung Fu Panda p.**135**
- Somewhere Between p.**183**
- St. Vincent p.**251**
- Teenage Mutant Ninja Turtles (2014 version) p.**159**

Birth Parents and Birth Family

- Antwone Fisher p.**214**
- Belle p.**217**
- Boxtrolls, The p.**111**
- Closure p.**166**
- Creed p.**170**
- Delivery Man p.**230**
- How to Train Your Dragon 2 p.**133**
- I Am Sam p.**233**
- Ida p.**237**
- Man of Steel p.**175**
- Kung Fu Panda 3 p.**141**
- Meet the Robinsons p.**80**
- Remember My Story: ReMoved Part 2 p.**248**
- Rio 2 p.**155**
- Somewhere Between p.**183**

- Star Wars: Episodes I–VI as a unit; individually, Episodes III, V, VI, and VII pp.**187–207**
- Tigger Movie, The p.**103**

Considering Adoption and Journeying Towards Adoption

- Big Daddy p.**219**
- Blind Side, The p.**223**
- Camp (2013 version) p.**226**
- Closure p.**166**
- Delivery Man p.**230**
- I Am Sam p.**233**
- Ida p.**237**
- Martian Child p.**240**
- Odd Life of Timothy Green, The p.**85**
- Remember My Story: ReMoved Part 2 p.**248**
- ReMoved p.**246**
- Somewhere Between p.**183**

Cross-Cultural Adoption

- Belle p.**217**
- Blind Side, The p.**223**
- Boxtrolls, The p.**111**
- Choose Your Own Adventure: The Abominable Snowman p.**115**
- Closure p.**166**
- Ernest and Celestine p.**129**
- Kung Fu Panda 2 p.**138**
- Kung Fu Panda 3 p.**141**
- Man of Steel p.**175**
- Mr. Peabody and Sherman p.**145**
- Paddington p.**149**
- Rio 2 p.**155**
- Somewhere Between p.**183**

Dad Adoption

Dealing with People Who Oppose Adoption

Divided Loyalties

Emotions

Family Defined

Family Formation

Fitting In and Belonging; Family Roles

Foster Care

- I Am Sam p.**233**
- Jungle Book, The (1967 version) p.**73**
- Lilo and Stitch p.**77**
- Martian Child p.**240**
- Moonrise Kingdom p.**243**
- Paddington p.**149**
- Remember My Story: ReMoved Part 2 p.**248**
- ReMoved p.**246**
- Secondhand Lions p.**179**

God in Adoption

- Camp (2013 version) p.**226**
- Somewhere Between p.**183**

Identity Development and Identity Shared Between Two Families

- Boxtrolls, The p.**111**
- Choose Your Own Adventure: The Abominable Snowman p.**115**
- Closure p.**166**
- Creed p.**170**
- Divergent p.**172**
- How to Train Your Dragon 2 p.**133**
- Ida p.**237**
- Kung Fu Panda 2 p.**138**
- Kung Fu Panda 3 p.**141**
- Man of Steel p.**175**
- Mr. Peabody and Sherman p.**145**
- Penguins of Madagascar p.**153**
- Remember My Story: ReMoved Part 2 p.**248**
- Rio 2 p.**155**
- Secondhand Lions p.**179**
- Somewhere Between p.**183**
- Star Wars: Episode I: The Phantom Menace p.**187**

Infertility

Loss

Maintaining Relationships Over Distance

Relative Adoption

Relinquishment

Reunion

Second Choices and Worries that Adoption Is a Second Choice

Secrets

Self-Acceptance

Self-Blame

Siblings

Single-Parent Adoptions

Social Workers

Therapy

Understanding Difficult or Confusing Behaviors

Waiting to Be Adopted

REFERENCES AND FURTHER READING

Ashton, S. (2016) *The Secrets of Successful Adoptive Parenting: Practical Advice and Strategies to Help with Emotional and Behavioural Challenges*. London: Jessica Kingsley Publishers.

Banish, R. with Jordan-Wong, J. (1992) *A Forever Family*. New York, NY: HarperCollins Children's.

Bond, J. with Goldman, C. (2016) *Jazzy's Quest: What Matters Most*. Jacksonville, FL: Marcinson Press.

Brodzinsky, A. (2013) *Can I tell you about Adoption? A guide for friends, family and professionals*. London: Jessica Kingsley Publishers.

Cole, J. (1999, first published 1995) *How I Was Adopted*. New York, NY: HarperCollins.

Donovan, S. (2013) *No Matter What: An Adoptive Family's Story of Hope, Love and Healing*. London: Jessica Kingsley Publishers.

Donovan, S. (2014) *The Unofficial Guide to Adoptive Parenting: The Small Stuff, The Big Stuff and The Stuff In Between*. London: Jessica Kingsley Publishers.

Goldman, C. with Bond, J. (2015) *Jazzy's Quest: Adopted and Amazing*. Jacksonville, FL: Marcinson Press.

Holden, L. and Hass, C. (2013) *The Open-Hearted Way to Open Adoption*. Lanham, MD: Rowman & Littlefield.

Jean, A., Reiss, M., Martin, J., Meyer, G. *et al.* (Writers) and Reardon, J. (Director) (1991) Treehouse of Horror II [Television series episode]. In A. Jean (Executive Producer), *The Simpsons*. Los Angeles, CA: 20th Century Fox Television.

Kasza, K. (1996, first published 1992) *A Mother for Choco.* New York, NY: Puffin.

Madigan, T. (2012) *I'm Proud of You: My Friendship with Fred Rogers.* Los Angeles, CA: Ubuntu Press.

Maslow, A. H. (1943) "A Theory of Human Motivation." *Psychological Review 50,* 4, 370–396.

Parr, T. (2007) *We Belong Together.* New York, NY: Little, Brown & Company.

Silverstein, D. N. and Kaplan, S. (no date, but drawing from their work originally published in 1982) Lifelong Issues in Adoption. Washington, DC: American Adoption Congress. Available at www.americanadoptioncongress.org/grief_silverstein_article.php, accessed on 24 September, 2016.

ACKNOWLEDGMENTS

This is a book about movies and conversations. Movies go hand in hand with long, rambling acknowledgment speeches and I've got lots of people that I'm thankful to and thankful for. No story is completed in isolation, much less a book about conversations. First, I'm thankful to God for providing health, opportunity, family, and friends. Throughout the writing of this book I've been supported, helped, and encouraged by some very good people. If you're one of them, thank you! I want to particularly thank a few of you.

- My wife, Noel, in you I've got a friend, a confidante, a great encourager, and someone to watch a lot of movies with. The fact that you're also a really solid editor is just extra awesomeness.

- My parents, Greg and Ruth Cooper, thanks for a lifetime of support. Your encouragement and guidance have been just as important to me as an adult as they were to me as a kid.

- Michael Mazur, thanks for believing in me, in this book, and in what I'm doing. Your guidance is so appreciated. I hope I'm as cool an uncle to my nieces and nephews as you are to me.

- Rachel, Michael, Molly, Amelia, Ella, and Adonai—thanks for loving me and letting me feel like a cool uncle.

- Larry, Martha, Holly, David, Emily, and Elijah (hello, hello, hello, goodbye!)—my in-laws. Thanks for making me a part of your family and for believing in this book.

- Bob and Sandy, thank you for claiming me as a grandson. I'm so grateful to God for your place in my family's life.

- Sean Love, thanks for your consistent encouragement, your insight into this book, the reminders to keep my life in balance, and being a really good friend.

- Andrew and Katie, Matt and Melody, and Joel and Heather—thanks for your great friendship.

- Rick and Vonnie, Eric and Nancy, and Montrose Church—Noel and I are pretty far from the East Coast. Thanks for helping California feel like home.

- Matt Baughman, thanks for encouraging me to write this, and for helping to create my first list of movies to review.

- Sarah DeHay, I'm so grateful for your support as I worked to finish this book. I've grown personally and professionally through knowing you.

- Elijah Davidson, thanks for hosting my very first posts on your site, *Reel Spirituality*, and for your input in developing the structure that I use in each review.

- Lori Holden, thanks for teaching me how to be a blogger and for modeling how to respond positively, even to hurtful comments.

- Linda Grobman, thanks for making me a columnist and for the great feedback on my first draft!

- Chris, Eve, Brianna, and Kim—thanks for providing space in your magazines for me to write about film and adoption.

- David Corey, Danielle McLean, Stephen Jones, and everyone else at Jessica Kingsley Publishers—thanks for believing in this book and giving me a chance to fulfill a long-held goal.

- To the many people who share their adoption stories through blogs or film, thank you for your openness. I have learned so much from you: Bryan and Angela Tucker, David and Urban Quint, Linda Goldstein Knowlton, Nathanael and Christina Matanick, Amanda Woolston, Laura Dennis, Kumar Jensen, and several others.

- I'm a social worker, but a few years ago I started being a film reviewer as well. It was kind of like being the new kid at a huge, somewhat intimidating school. I'm so thankful to Nathan Marcy at Fox, Lindsay Kwek at Paramount, Marshall Weinbaum at Disney, Tara McNamara at That Was Something, and Emily McDonald at Acme PR for treating me so kindly. You've encouraged me by validating the work I'm doing and have helped me feel like I belong. Thank you. You're excellent at what you do.

- Noel, Greg, Ruth Ann, Rachel, Michael, Molly, Amelia, Ella, Adonai, Michael, Larry, Martha, Holly, David, Emily, Elijah, Bob, Sandy, Rob, Beth, Michael, Becky, John, Rebecca, Jenna, Madeline, Samantha, Sarah, Nate, Paul, Gloria, Marie, Gary, Evelyn, Mike, Ray, Bobbi, Vicki, Diana, Erin, Alexa, Taylor, Andrew, Joel, Aaron, Angel, Rhonda, Bea, Stanley, Mark, Teckla, Peter, Teresa, Claude, Katie, Dylan, Vanessa, Dallas, and everybody else—thanks for being my family.

Addison Cooper is the primary established film reviewer for the adoption community.

His website, Adoption at the Movies (www.adoptionatthemovies.com), is visited 20,000 times each month, and he has also written about film for five niche magazines directed to foster care and adoption audiences. Addison is a regular columnist for *The New Social Worker* magazine and a licensed clinical social worker in both California and Missouri. He has ten years of experience in the adoption world as a social worker, therapist, and supervisor, and has helped finalize the adoptions of 100 children out of foster care. Addison lives in California, USA.